Everybody Wants To Go To Heaven

6 Steps to
Organizational
Excellence

Patrick J. McDonnell

Retired Partner, Former Vice Chairman Business Assurance,
Coopers & Lybrand LLP

© 2002 Patrick J. McDonnell

Cover designed by Roberta Dickinson
Edited by Dorri Jacobs

Library of Congress Control Number: 2002110013

Publisher's Cataloging-in-Publication
(Provided by Quality Books, Inc.)

McDonnell, Patrick J.
    Everybody wants to go to Heaven : six steps to
organizational excellence / Patrick J. McDonnell. -- 1st
ed.
    p. cm.
    ISBN 978-0-615-18943-7

    1. Industrial management. 2. Organizational
effectiveness. 3. Organizational change.   I. Title.

HD31.M33 2002   658
                        QBI02-200535

Contents

Preface

This book is for *you*—a person of intelligence and character who wishes to lead your organization to excellence.

Learning its lessons will enable you to effect the behavioral change needed to achieve your objective. They were learned over thirty years of directing and advising diverse organizations in achieving organizational excellence.

Along the way, I learned several important lessons. First, the objective of all change programs is to achieve excellence. Nothing less is worth the effort. Second, there is a process whose principles can be applied to achieve excellence. Third, the process is universally applicable. Fourth, these principles are timeless—a constant in a world of change. And, finally, anyone with the willingness to understand the process and the courage to implement it can be successful.

This process—Six Steps to Organizational Excellence—is the subject of this book. Many excellent books have been written on motivating, planning, strategy, leadership and selling. It is not my intent to replicate them. What I am trying to do is place these subjects in a context, so that you may understand their role in creating excellence.

Many books have also been written about the *change process*. Most tell you *what* to do. This book tells you *how* to do it.

This book is organized to lead you through each of the Six Steps:

- **Introduction:** *Your Six Steps to Heaven.*
The principles of the Six Step Process.

- **Step 1**: *Master Change.*
The importance of motivation. Common negative reactions to change and how to overcome them.

- **Step 2**: *Build a Values-Based Community.*
The importance of trust and its role in achieving excellence.

- **Step 3**: *Lead More Effectively.*
The principles of leadership and their role in creating a values-based community.

- **Step 4**: *Create a Strategic Plan.*
The fundamentals of strategic planning: Evaluating your strategic environment, setting strategic goals and organizing to achieve them. Introduces the concepts of value drivers and business processes and their role in achieving excellence.

- **Step 5:** *Execute Your Plan.*
Effect change by executing your plan. Enhance the quality of your value drivers. Achieve excellence by becoming the employer of choice to the best people and the company of choice to the best customers.

Case studies are provided to facilitate your understanding. There are two case studies:

LSB&G Achieves Excellence illustrates the Six Step Process applied in a professional services environment.

HlthCo Achieves Excellence illustrates the universal applicability of the Six Step Process.

• **Step 6**: *Achieve Continuous Improvement.*
Explains how to achieve continuous improvement, the perpetual motion machine of organizational excellence.

This book was written for you, the CEO, (Chief Executive Officer), and for your management team, because you are either effecting change, contemplating it, or should be contemplating it. It is for anyone who is subjected to change or who aspires to a position of leadership. Finally, it is for entrepreneurs faced with the challenge of managing rapid growth.

Successfully effecting change is a skill, and those who master the lessons of this book will differentiate themselves.

The focus here is on leadership—not management. Leadership encompasses management, because accomplishing objectives requires mastering management skills—planning, organizing, budgeting and monitoring. But managing is not leading. Organizations consist of people and people must be led. Leadership skills extend to the human element, causing people to willingly execute their leader's vision. The Six Step Process explains the role of leadership and facilitates its development.

Many people recognize the need for change and appreciate the merits of the Six Step Process but do not feel empowered to implement it. Their rationale is that they cannot do enough to change their environment. My response to those who feel that way is this. Start the revolution and watch it spread. Begin by developing your leadership skills. Use them to improve your effectiveness and help your colleagues do the same. Speak up. Question why. Seek improvement. Commit yourself to personal excellence. Learn to lead. Learn to win. Soon you—and then your colleagues—will gain a reputation for excellence that others will try to emulate.

That is how I began. I was not trying to start a revolution. I was merely trying to help colleagues and clients become more efficient and effective. As my accomplishments became evident, I was given the opportunity to effect change in ever more challenging situations. Eventually, the changes I led had global ramifications.

The lessons of this book are universally applicable, because change is about the way individuals react and behave, and the one element common to all organizations is people.

Much of my career was spent with Coopers & Lybrand (hereafter referred to as "the Firm" or "our Firm"), one of the Big Six accounting, audit and consulting firms. In 1998, it merged with Price Waterhouse to form PricewaterhouseCoopers (the "merged Firm").

I have seen many management trends, but the principles of the Six Step Process are timeless. My business career began in the Age of Aquarius—the era of "doing your own thing" and being a "people person." Management encouraged the unlimited expression of individuality. *Touchy-feely* was the name of the game.

Feeling good was the objective.

This sense of individualism evolved into an era of collegiality, where the old style "command and control" manager became a "facilitator" whose objective was to ensure that before any decisions were made, all concerns were addressed.

Consensus was the objective.

In the more recent "New Economy," an era of youthful leaders, entrepreneurs and new technologies, the role of leadership, strategic planning, organization and return on investment were viewed as obsolete. My dot-com colleagues explained that the Six Steps were definitely "Old Economy." Besides, implementing them would take much too long.

Short-term results were the objective.

With the crash of the dot-bombs, the fallacy of this fad has become apparent—just as have those that preceded it.

In navigating the management fad minefields, I learned that change is constant and that fads will come and go. But those who practice the Six Step Process will consistently achieve organizational excellence.

One example, in particular, is a software company upon whose board I sit. This publicly held company with revenues of $70 million began in the basement of its founder and CEO. Throughout turbulent times, customer demands, management fads and challenging competitors, the CEO remained committed to the principles of the Six Step Process. He is the epitome of values-based leadership. Fads come and go. Substance does not.

As I write this, I'm in my late fifties, perhaps ancient by some measures, certainly old school by most. I'm just old enough to know what I am talking about, yet young enough to continue learning, as I practice what I am about to preach. Keep my perspective in mind as you read, as I refer to historical figures, books and personal experiences that may have occurred before you were born.

You may consider some of my opinions difficult to accept—or inconsistent with your own. So be it.

Consider them in the spirit in which they are offered—to impart the lessons of a business career devoted to achieving excellence.

Embrace them or reject them in whole or in part. That is your choice. That is also the nature of learning. So keep an open mind.

This book will either reinforce that which you already know or expose you to points of view you have not yet considered. Either way, I am confident that it will stimulate your thinking and contribute to your success.

Acknowledgments

I began this book over a year ago. The first draft was written in three weeks, and I assumed it would be on the street shortly thereafter. Fortunately, thanks to the following people, that didn't happen.

I owe this book primarily to my publisher, Rachel Rapoport, and my editor, Dr. Dorri Jacobs. The fact that Dorri and I are still speaking is testimony to our mutual respect. Her professionalism and patient, yet persistent insistence that I could do better caused me to try. While she deserves the most credit, there are others as well. Rich Baird and Gail Palmer, colleagues and advisors for many years refreshed my memory, and tactfully told me to listen to Dorri.

I wish to thank other friends and colleagues— Retired Army Colonel and President of Colorado Christian College Larry Donnithorne, author and entrepreneur Dr. Brooks Mitchell, consultant and author Charles Poirier, Senior Managing Director of RSM McGladrey, Inc. Mark Scally, Bill Stone, CEO of SS&C Technologies, Inc., and author Bill Ury of Harvard Law School—who read the manuscript and provided suggestions.

Writing a book of life experiences caused me to reflect upon those who provided them. Time and space precludes listing them all, but some stand out.

My friend and Company Commander, John Heller, exemplified Marine Corps leadership. At Coopers & Lybrand, a number of partners, especially Jim Meehan, Vin O'Reilly, Ed Premo, Bill Richards, Karl Scharff, Bob Siskin, Marty Westfall—and especially, Former Chairman of Coopers & Lybrand Gene Freedman—were mentors, friends and role models. To them I am indebted for their interest and support.

I owe my greatest thanks to my wife, confidante, chief counselor and best friend, Michaele Ann, who lived through it all and without whose love, patience and support I could not have been successful. She has been there for me—and for our sons—every step of the way. She has my love and gratitude.

Because of them, and many others, this book is a reality.

To Michaele Ann, my wife and best friend,
to those who taught me professionalism,
to those who taught me the business,
to those who taught me leadership and
to those who left it better than they found it.

Introduction:

Your Six Steps to Heaven

Everybody wants to go to Heaven—but nobody wants to die!

Nobody seems to know much about Heaven —what it looks like or even where it is. Yet we seem to agree that it's good and we want to go there. The only problem with going to Heaven, of course, is the need to die to get there. That seems to be a pretty steep price. Organizational excellence has similar attributes. We all want it, yet few of us can define it.

Achieving excellence requires acting differently. That means *change*, which is often considered a pretty steep price to pay for achieving *anything*. Change may not be as dramatic as death, but at times may seem like it.

The good news? You don't need to die to get to the Heaven of Organizational Excellence. All you need to do is to implement the Six Step Process.

It is the yellow brick road to Heaven.

The Nature of Change

Change falls into two categories—strategic and tactical.

Strategic change has broad, substantive, irreversible impact. It may include your company's financial turnaround, the transformation of its structure and reporting relationships, divesting a major segment of your business or merging with another entity.

Tactical change is either inherent in effecting strategic change or is an independent event. For example, you might adopt new policies and procedures, outsource business functions, develop marketing plans, consolidate, downsize or expand operating units, implement a new computer system or introduce new products and services.

The Six Step Process is applicable in effecting strategic or tactical change.

Early in my business career, I realized that, apart from my professional accounting skills, I was really in the change *leadership* business—both in serving clients and within the Firm. While my clients were faced with shifting market demands, new competitors and turnover of personnel, the accounting profession was being challenged as well.

Public accounting was once a dignified profession. Clients rarely changed affiliation. Business development was conducted in a discrete manner. Then, as clients perceived that switching firms would reduce fees, it evolved into a dogfight. Our margins eroded as we incurred the expense required to remain competitive. We needed to *change* the way we did business.

In this environment, because of interest and developing ability, I was generally assigned to new and/or troubled clients. Serving them developed skills in problem analysis, decision-making, negotiation, communication and, above all, leadership.

I learned that these skills are required to effect change. Unlike many, I thrived—and became skilled at deriving order from the many crises I encountered.

My change leadership skills improved in managing organizations within the Firm, all of which had fallen short of financial and quality standards. Over time, I found that the size of these organizations increased—from $10 million in revenue to $1.25 billion—but the process of restoring them to excellence remained the same.

More recent experiences in a variety of industries confirm that belief.

I found it enormously satisfying to see organizations—and the people that comprise them—rise from chaos and experience the joys of excellence.

The ability to effect positive change is a rewarding and value-adding skill that must be mastered by those who aspire to leadership in virtually any organization.

I have endeavored to enhance these skills throughout my career. Courtesy of the Marine Corps, I benefited from a three-year education in the theory and practice of leadership. But, as much as I knew about leadership and its relationship to effecting change, I realized that there was much to be learned from those whose lives had been committed to change.

I have always been a reader—mostly history, sports, biographies and the usual dose of business books. Most have influenced me. I also sought the advice of—and observed—CEO friends, clients, colleagues and others whose leadership styles I sought to emulate. I spent a great deal of time thinking about the subject. These readings, conversations and observations—as tested against the experiences of a thirty-year business career—evolved into the Six Steps to Organizational Excellence.

I encourage you to develop your ability to extract key information from many sources in formulating your own opinions and developing your unique style.

We Have All Been There

In many ways, we begin our journey from a common perspective. Although you may not have experienced *successful* change, you have experienced change. Perhaps the following scenario sounds familiar. You may have been in the audience. Or perhaps you were at the podium.

The auditorium is packed. The CEO at the podium waits for the buzz to die down. Balloons hang from the ceiling. Banners are ready. This is the big day—the day we launch the long-awaited *change program*.

Finally, the room settles down to hear the CEO's words of wisdom and hope. Things here at Global Colossal Technologies, Inc. have not been going well. Growth is lagging, margins are eroding and we are losing some of our best people. But this is the day we initiate the turnaround.

The CEO smooths his steel gray hair, looks them in the eye and says, "Who's ready for *growth*?" People begin to twitter. "Who's ready to *leapfrog our competition?*" A few feeble "yeahs" begin to emerge. In a louder voice, the CEO asks, "Who's ready to be the *best in this business*?" "Yeah, Boss, we are," booms the crowd.

Now he pours it on. "Who's ready to *see our stock soar*? Who's ready to get *rich*?"

The "yeahs" approach hysteria. At the peak of evangelical frenzy, he asks, "If *rich* is your idea of Heaven—who wants *to go to Heaven?*"

The crowd goes nuts. *"We do! We do! We want to go to Heaven,"* they scream.

The band begins to play. "Be the Best" balloons float from the ceiling, while the banners unfurl. Hysteria reaches a crescendo, while the CEO beams his approval.

At last, the crowd settles down to await more good news. The CEO looks out and, with a concerned expression on his deeply tanned face, says, "Now, who's ready to *change* the way we do business around here?" The response is, "Huh?"

"Who's ready to commit to *changing the way we do our jobs every day?*" The "yeahs" have been replaced with stony silence and a few scattered "Whadesays?" "Who's ready to lead the *change charge?*" he asks.

The reaction in the now quiet crowd is "Fuhgeddaboudit."

The CEO understands the first maxim of the change game. *Everybody wants to go to Heaven—but nobody wants to die!* He knows that everybody is excited about the benefits of change—as long as someone else is doing the changing.

He's not deterred. He juts out his chiseled jaw and in a soothing voice says, "Don't worry. I know that change is challenging, and we're prepared. I have appointed Joe Newguy, our newest junior vice president, to assume the position of VP of Cultural Change and lead us through this challenging process. Backing up Newguy will be Letz, Cheatem & Goode, world-class change management consultants. By the way, don't forget your T-shirts as you leave. We must all be *change agents!*"

With that, he appeals for buy-in, turns to Newguy and says, "Okay, Newguy, you've got the ball. Any time you need help, just call." Basking in a glow of self-satisfaction and with faint applause ringing in his ears, the CEO hurries off for a few days of golf. Within weeks, his picture will be on the cover of business magazines, touting his "dynamic vision" and skills as a "change agent."

You know the rest of the story. In less than six months, Newguy and the consultants will be history.

And the CEO will blame the failure of his change program on "ingrained culture."

Sound familiar?

The CEO didn't get much right, but he at least understands the dynamics of the change conflict. Everybody supports the benefits of reducing staff—provided it is not *your* staff being reduced. Heaven is great, but I'm not willing to die getting there.

In fairness, the CEO demonstrated responsibility. Effecting positive change is not an option for organizational leadership. *It is their primary responsibility.*

He also provided a key element of successful change—a statement of his vision for the organization. Vision is the leader's definition of a future state—a condition worth achieving. Vision involves *what* the organization should be. Strategy and its objectives, which relate to *how* the vision is to be realized, will be discussed later. The CEO's vision was the "Heaven" of economic benefit—*being* rich. His strategy—how he was going to get there—was ill-defined and poorly supported. And that is why he failed.

This is why most change initiatives fail. It takes more than articulating a vision to create it. A strategy and proactive leadership are required to implement it. Vision is meaningless without commitment and the ability to realize it.

The CEO was also right about the dynamics. It is naïve to do the same things in the same way, yet expect a different result. To achieve a different result, you must do something different. You must change.

This means challenging everything you do. Begin by asking why you are doing it. If your answer is "Because that's the way we've always done it," you are in a position to effect positive change. Compare everything you are doing against the standard of doing it better, faster and more cost-effectively. Then organize, motivate and lead your organization to achieve a higher standard of excellence.

The good news? You *can* realize your vision. You can go to Heaven—and you don't need to die getting there. "Heaven," as used here, means organizational excellence, because without it, the long-term viability of your company is in jeopardy. Besides, what else is worth the effort? Realizing that vision—*becoming* excellent—is an intense process, fraught with frustration and risk. It involves—and relies upon—behavioral change. It can be done, provided you commit yourself to the principles described here.

Producing change is *not* the objective of this book. The objective is Heaven—strategic excellence. Achieving it requires being absolutely excellent at *everything* you do. It means being the absolute *best* at whatever you are trying to achieve. Your goal—regardless of the organization for which you are responsible, or of which you are a member—is to be the *best* at whatever you are empowered or expected to do. Nothing less is acceptable. Nothing less is worth the effort.

The Six Step Process

Getting to Heaven requires change. And the Six Step Process will take you there by *creating* the changes in behavior needed to achieve excellence. There are no shortcuts to Heaven. You must follow the Six Steps to Organizational Excellence carefully—and in sequence:

First: *Master change.*

Understand motivation—the factors that make us behave as we do. Frustrations, fears and anxieties characterize each individual's reactions to change.

This response—and the environment it produces—is a "Valley of Death" that you must navigate. Understand measurement, because you will get what you measure and nothing else. Finally, use the Six Step Process as a competitive differentiator.

Second: *Build a values-based community.*

Trust is the key to behavioral change. Trust is created only in a community based upon commonly held and respected values.

Third: *Lead more effectively.*

Everything depends on this. Practice principled problem-solving and participative decision-making, which will create and sustain an environment of trust.

Fourth: *Create a strategic plan.*

Begin by articulating a vision—a view of the future to be attained. Then relate that vision to strategic objectives which are based upon an assessment of your environment. Create an organization to implement your plan. Align organizational and personal objectives. Identify value drivers—those factors inherent in every organization whose improvement will create excellence. Understand business processes—the policies, practices and procedures that collectively impact value drivers. Identify the ones that support value drivers.

Fifth: *Execute your plan.*

Execute your strategic plan by improving the effectiveness of business processes. Redesign them when appropriate, to improve overall effectiveness and efficiency.

Sixth: *Achieve continuous improvement.*

This is the endgame—the perpetual motion machine of organizational excellence. When you have done that, you will have reached Heaven. Your journey will be complete.

You may be wondering, is the Six Step Process the only path to Heaven? There may be many ways to achieve strategic excellence, but only one is of interest here—the best way.

Some CEO clients have challenged my assertion that the Six Step Process is the best approach. Their argument is, "There are many ways to create change. How can you be so certain that your process is the best?"

They generally dismiss the need for motivation, the role of a values-based community or creating proactive leadership, considering these to be a given. Their focus is on Step Four, strategic planning. They soon have their organization immersed in planning books, subcommittees, consultants, deadlines and even "Be the Best" shirts.

In rushing to Step Four—akin to building a house without a foundation—these clients make a common mistake. Then, when their houses fall over, they cannot understand why.

I do not suggest that the Six Step Process is the *only* way, I merely maintain it is the *best* way.

The uniqueness of the Six Steps is the emphasis on *process*—beginning with the First Step and ending with the Sixth. The Process is relatively simple, but the steps are interrelated and must be followed in sequence. No shortcuts or ducking the tough stuff.

The road to Heaven—organizational excellence —is right there before you.

Just follow it.

CHECKPOINTS on the Road to Heaven

For a leader, effecting positive change is not an option. It is your primary responsibility. The objective of change is to create organizational excellence. Nothing else is worth the effort.

Let's review the Six Step Process:

The Six Step Process

1. Master change.
2. Build a values-based community.
3. Lead more effectively.
4. Create a strategic plan.
5. Execute your plan.
6. Achieve continuous improvement.

The need for change is inherent in any organization. To ignore it ensures the inevitable failure of that organization.

Most CEOs understand this. Too few understand how to do it successfully.

Begin your own assessment of the need for change by answering these questions:

- Where will your organization be in 5 years?
- What will it look like?

- What will it have accomplished?

- What is your vision of the future?

- How well do your people understand that vision?

- How have you articulated a strategy to realize your vision?

- Are you prepared to lead in implementing that strategy?

- If not you, then who?

The road to Heaven begins with an honest assessment of your own need for—and ability to —change. Begin by questioning everything you are doing:

- How receptive are you to new ideas?

- Do you foster change in your organization?

- Why do you do it this way?

- Why do you do it at all?

- How could it be done better, faster, cheaper or most cost-effectively?

- What are the dynamics of your industry?

- What are your competitors doing?

The Six Steps are interrelated and must be followed in sequence. Remember the importance of motivation, creating a values-based community and being a principled, sensitive leader.

These factors must be addressed *before* your planning process begins. To do otherwise ensures that the journey to the Heaven of Organizational Excellence will be long, bumpy and likely to end in failure.

This has been an overview of the Six Steps to Organizational Excellence. Now it's time to discuss each step in detail, beginning with Step One—Master change.

Step One

Master Change

*The journey to the Heaven of Organizational Excellence
begins with taking the first step.*

Your journey begins with changing your own behavior and that of others. You must understand your challenge. Creating substantive, positive change is rarely successful. Considerable time, money, human resources and energy are usually spent with marginal results. As a leader of change, your risk is high and failure cannot be an option. Fortunately, the Six Step Process ensures success.

Begin the journey by understanding the fundamentals of motivation.

Motivation

Why should you change the way you are doing business? You're doing okay. The company is making money. Your people seem satisfied. Your customers are paying on time, so they must be satisfied. You just *know* you are better than your competitors. So why risk all of this to change? As the old adage goes, if it ain't broke, why fix it?

Be wary of jumping to conclusions. Instead, consider these questions:

- Are you sure your customers and people are satisfied?

- How do you know?

- Have you surveyed your major constituencies—your employees, customers, vendors and shareholders?

- What do they tell you?

- Do the best people want to work for you?

- Do you attract and keep the best customers?

- Are you *feared* by your competitors?

- Are you acknowledged as the best in your industry by the trade press?

You'd better find out the answers and respond appropriately. The alternative to change is business as usual. And *that* is high-risk in a constantly changing marketplace. If you were so naïve as to assume long-term status quo in your industry, you would not be in your job. It is far more likely that you *know* that you must move your organization forward. But how will you motivate your people to change? What can you do to make them aware of the threats and opportunities? These are important questions.

You're not the first executive to face that challenge. Consider this statement by a CEO that appeared as an advertisement in *The Wall Street Journal*.[1]

> To build a firm clients want to work with, we built a firm where people want to work. . . Being an employer of choice means creating innovative human resource programs that meet professional needs and provide professional fulfillment. Only then can we provide top drawer service to our clients.

---

[1] *The Wall Street Journal*, March 21, 2001.

There are only two possible conclusions that can be inferred from his pronouncement. He could be declaring victory. The firm *is* an employer of choice, one with which clients want to work, and it *does* provide top-drawer service. If so, I envy them. This is a pretty bold assertion of organizational excellence.

On the other hand, it could be a vision statement—a CEO's call to arms. The real message is "We had better become an employer of choice and a firm our clients want to work with—or we're toast." The CEO is challenging his people to become excellent.

Either way, the firm now has three choices. First, it can do nothing. After all, they've done it. They are the best. Forget new ideas. If it really *was* a good idea, they would have thought of it years ago. The fact that they don't do it that way means it can't be a good idea. As ridiculous as that sounds, I have heard fundamentally the same argument many times —usually from an arrogant, successful entity about to enter its death spiral.

If in fact they *are* the best, they are faced with a second choice—implementing a program to maintain their status. Being Number One is tough. Competing CEOs use your position to motivate their own people. You are in everyone's sights and they're just waiting for you to become sufficiently complacent to knock you off.

Finally—and more likely—they are *not* the best. Their CEO is giving them a wake-up call to initiate the Six Step Process or be left in the competitive dust. This is an excellent strategy. The CEO of Global Colossal Technologies used it to deliver his message. So can you.

The call to arms entails risk. It is the corporate equivalent of burning the boats. Once begun, the process must end in only one of two ways: success

—getting to Heaven—or failure, which may be worse than doing nothing.

I first learned this lesson as a young partner when our Chairman sent each of us an excellent book that was the buzz of America's boardrooms. I read it in eager anticipation of the firm-wide initiative that would surely follow to implement its lessons. Nothing happened. In terms of motivating us, he would have been better off not having sent it at all. By sending it, he indicated that we must change—and set forth a vision of what we needed to become. But he failed to follow up with a strategy to implement this vision. The result was a loss of confidence in his ability to lead.

Your call to arms must be nothing less than a first step in *implementing* the Six Step Process. Otherwise, the cynical backlash of doing nothing will deprive you of your last best chance to achieve excellence.

Faced with the risk of *doing nothing* or the *risk* of acting, which do you choose? Which is the *lesser* of these two evils: going up the change hill—knowing you will lose a *few* people—or staying at the status quo bottom and eventually losing *all* of your people?

As the opening salvo in implementing the Six Step Process, the call to arms has been my preferred method. It gets attention. It is dramatic and demands a response. "Are we the best or aren't we?" causes the issues to be articulated. It facilitates communication. Above all, it causes people to decide. Are they going to risk charging up the change hill or accept the consequences of hiding at the bottom?

Detect or stimulate factors that will motivate your organization to initiate change. Often the circumstances are external and evident—a competitive threat, financial underperformance, loss of revenue, key people or customers. Here the rallying call is relatively easy.

What if the factors are less apparent? My arrival as the managing partner in a large office was once met with the arrogance of the uninformed. The office had been profitable but underperforming for many years. So my call to arms was met with anger and resentment. My approach was to provide them with facts. I compared their performance with that of ten peer offices over the previous five years. Their relative underperformance was clearly evident. Now armed with reality, we began our journey to Heaven.

Your organization cannot begin the journey to Heaven without the motivation to do so.

From Psychology 101, you will recall the fundamentals of motivation—generally summarized as *survival, security* and *self-actualization.*[2] Over the years, I have come to define these motivators as *fear, greed* and *pride.* To effect change, you must understand how they motivate human behavior.

Fear. How about fear? What's wrong with sweaty palms or a good kick in the head? It gets attention—but does not encourage a positive response. How do you react to bullies whose message is "Do it or else"? Does their behavior enhance your commitment? Your productivity? Your loyalty? Not likely.

Fear can stimulate positive behavior. Concern that "If we don't do something about our human resource programs, we won't have the right kind of people around here" calls attention to a critical issue.

Fear, in certain circumstances, is beneficial—but not a long-term motivator. "Do it or else" is negative reinforcement and contrary to human nature. It's okay to bolt for the door when the place is on fire, but people of substance do not allow themselves to be motivated by threats. If fear is your favorite

---

[2] Peter M. Serge, *The Fifth Discipline Fieldbook: The Art and Practice of the Learning Organization* (New York: Doubleday, 1994), 24.

form of motivation, you use it at great risk to your career and to the welfare of your company.

Greed. Greed also has its advantages. Be honest. We're all a little bit greedy. Who doesn't want a better lifestyle and more toys? Motivation by greed, though, is high risk, because it encourages self-centered behavior. Greed's focus generally isn't on making the trough bigger. It's on elbowing your way to more of the slop. Team compensation is a tactic often used to increase the size of the trough. But even in team situations, the individual eye is on enlarging the personal share of the team rewards. If not managed, those motivated by greed will not only eat the slop, they will eat the trough.

Pride. Finally, we come to pride. When you walk the dusty streets of the marketplace, you want your competitors to get off the sidewalk and cower in the doorways. You want the best-looking clients fluttering their eyelashes when you walk in the room. You want your suppliers to wag their tails and bow-wow at the mere thought of doing business with you.

There is nothing more effective than pride as a motivator. What causes Marines to crawl through terrorist-filled tunnels? Fear? Their only fear is failing to live their esprit de corps. What compels fire fighters and police officers to charge into burning buildings? The stock option plan? More likely, it is their fierce pride in being members of a values-based community.

Pride is not to be confused with running around screaming, "We're Number One" when your 2 and 6 team scores a touchdown. Pride is substantive. Consider the great institutions—religions, countries, armies, companies, football teams and great universities, including your alma mater. Their common characteristic is pride—in their values and in the community they created.

I once assisted a small, entrepreneurial, rapidly growing manufacturing company to achieve excellence. Like many similar companies, its internal procedures have not kept pace with growth. Inefficiency has eliminated profits. There are no bonuses. The risk of product failure is growing. If costs were not reduced, the company would not survive. We began the journey to excellence by improving cash flow. *Fear and greed work.*

With the cash crisis resolved, I asked management to describe the quality of their product. "It is excellent," I was told. "Best in the industry." "How then," I asked, "can you presume to produce excellence, if you are not excellent internally?" They were embarrassed, but agreed with my assessment of their processes. Their damaged pride is now motivating the achievement of excellence throughout the company.

Pride results from consistent focus on the factors that produce excellence—character, commitment to core values, dedicated leadership, development of skills, personal recognition and consistently winning.

Pride cannot exist in an atmosphere of fear and personal, financial or economic need. These needs must be addressed before anyone can be expected to focus on developing the pride needed to achieve and sustain excellence.

Because of its unique ability as a long-term motivator, creating pride is a primary objective of the Six Step Process.

It's Human Nature to Resist Change

Be forewarned. Changing behavior is not for the faint-hearted. In spite of your powers of persuasion and a heavy dose of positive motivation, it's human nature to resist change. You will cause discomfort, create stress and disrupt the routine of your colleagues. You are pushing them *outside their comfort zone.* They will let you know that this is not appreciated. If you want love, buy a dog. You will not get it from those subjected to your change initiative.

Human behavior is based on eons of relating actions with results. You touch the hot stove, you get burned. A leap of faith is required to change behavior without understanding the consequences. "Trust me, Og," says the clan leader. "My new spear makes mammoth killing a snap. Here. Go ahead and try it on that big fella over there." Og has just discovered the risk inherent in changing a familiar habit or practice.

Thanks to Og, human nature reflects certain characteristics that you—as the leader of change —must understand.

Typically, your people are conservative, honest and bright, excellent risk evaluators, but risk averse. They are experts on most things, regardless of experience. Give them enough time and they will talk themselves out of anything. Great at expressing concerns, they never have enough time or information—their favorite tactic is to create a committee to look into it and report back.

Don't agree? Try this. Gather your team together and say, "I've got good news. We've stacked the hall knee deep in thousand dollar bills. All you need to do when I give the word is take these bags, go out there and stuff them full of money. Whaddayasay?"

You will see wheels turning as they consider your proposal. Finally, someone will say impatiently, "I don't have time for that. I'm too busy serving our customers!" Then the office articulator of concerns will speak up. "I'm concerned about the health implications of all that green dye. Can you assure us we won't get agent orange disease?" "He's right," another may add. Their resistance begins to build. The self-appointed shop steward will ask, "What about our workers? Have we considered the impact on them of this action?"

And so it goes. By the time they're finished, they will have decided that they don't have enough information to make this decision. A committee will be appointed to look into it and report back. Meanwhile they all hurry back to their offices to read e-mails, while competitors grab the money.

The Valley of Death

Experience has taught me that there are generally five stages of reaction to the prospect of change. They are *denial, fear, anger, resignation* and finally, *triumph*.

I refer to the journey—from the first stage down the slope to stage two, hitting the bottom at stage three, crawling back up the other side to stage four and emerging at stage five—as traversing the *Valley of Death*. The road to Heaven runs right through the Valley. There is no going around it.

It's a long journey from stage one to stage five:

Stage 1: Denial.

"This too shall pass" is a typical initial reaction when someone learns of a prospective change program. "We've seen these change fads come and go," say the old corporate warriors. "If we just keep our heads down and ignore it, it'll go away."

Stage 2: Fear.

But what if it doesn't? You'll hear, "We don't have time to complete our work now, how can they expect us to do this too?" People see the prospect of change as a personal threat. So they resist. You are approaching the bottom of the Valley of Death.

Stage 3: Anger.

With the change initiative not dying as expected, fear gives way to anger. This is usually expressed as criticism, both of the plan and those who present it. The credibility, motivation and personal characteristics of change leaders are attacked. Critics point out flaws, expressing concerns about the plan's ramifications or problems with its implementation. Their objective is to poke enough holes in the plan dike to cause a break that will obliterate the plan and those who sponsor it. You have reached the bottom of the Valley of Death.

At this point, your courage, commitment and patience are essential. As fears are fed from the rumor mill, morale plummets and operations are disrupted. Negotiation and politics rear their ugly heads as everyone seeks a safe conduct pass. People will rationalize their resistance, "After all, these new policies can't apply to me. I'm the company's top producer in Buffalo."

Stage 4: Resignation.

Eventually, as you patiently implement the Six Step Process, continue to articulate the future, explain the need to change, invite feedback, listen and respond to appropriate concerns—and as your commitment becomes more apparent, employee resignation and commitment become evident. You are emerging from the Valley of Death.

Hold the celebration. You are still a long way from victory. Now is the time to redouble the effort. The change message must continue to be positive and directed personally and specifically at your best people. No matter how intense their reactions, be confident that if your message for change is substantive, the *best* people will agree with you. To build momentum, look to their support. When they are convinced of your commitment, they will provide it.

Stage 5: Triumph.

Your leadership and the substance of your message will build support for the change initiative. Fortunately, it takes only a relatively small number—not more than 20 to 25 percent of the best people rallying to the cause—to generate momentum. Focus your message and efforts on this group. The rest will come along in due course. If not, deal with them then. Avoid any pressure to respond to the ten percent who do not support change—and never will.

Navigating the Valley of Death

There is only one way through the Valley of Death—your leadership and commitment in implementing the Six Step Process. Navigating the Valley of Death requires a leap of faith on the part of your people. And taking this leap requires them to trust in your leadership. The Six Step Process is your guide to creating this environment of trust.

Failure is not an option. You will not fail if you stay the course and stick with the program. Be visible and continuously communicate. Appeal to your best people. Reinforce the positive aspects of the change. Tactfully, yet firmly, confront the inevitable problems and challenges—both political and personal. Above all, convey confidence and commitment.

You must lead, or the process will fail.

I have spent much of my career traversing the Valley of Death. My experiences are typical of the challenges and stress that characterize the Valley.

Some years ago, our Chairman initiated a strategic re-examination of our Firm. Its purpose was to correct a common problem in geographically oriented busi-nesses—an inappropriate amount of power at the lo-cal level—in our case, six geographic regions. A lack of cooperation had begun to adversely affect our per-formance. I had just been appointed as manager of one of the largest and more underperforming regions.

My difficulties began in the change sessions. I soon found that while I was implementing the Six Step Process in a region that desperately needed it—and was beginning to see results—nothing I sug-gested was well received. In fact, it was usually criti-cized in a patronizing manner. Thinking *outside the box* was encouraged—until you did it.

In retrospect, the situation was not difficult to understand. The party line was "Regional Manage-ment is the problem"—which, to some extent, was true. Nothing *any of us* said could be right. The more I attempted to explain my views, the more I was ad-monished, "Stop being defensive." When I tried to push my colleagues beyond their comfort zone, they resented it.

I felt angry and frustrated at having my ideas and experiences treated with so little respect. In a very short time, I was labeled "a problem," "someone who resists change" and "not a team player." Through the counseling of senior mentors, I eventually calmed down and it had a happy ending. But this was not my finest hour. In retrospect, it was a classic case of mis-communication.

This painful experience taught me several things. I learned to control my emotions—which I have endeavored to do since then, with various de-grees of success and some notable failures. More im-portantly, I learned empathy—my obligation to un-derstand the impact of change upon those involved. People act as they do for a reason. As a leader, you have an obligation to determine the reason, rather than merely react to it.

I learned to confront problems by meeting with those expressing frustration. People do *not* want to be pushed outside their comfort zone. Your goal is to understand why they are resistant and then mitigate it. It is amazing what you can discover when you ask—and the results you get when you listen to and address individual fears. Usually, you will gain the loyalty, respect and support of those who previously were your most vocal critics. At worst, they'll respect you for listening.

Change is stressful. Expect your colleagues to display a spectrum of emotions when facing it. Don't be surprised or react with anger, impatience or frustration, for their reactions are normal. This does not mean that you allow their negative responses to prevail. Generally, the most vocal are the most insecure, but their attitude does not represent the majority.

Patient and persistent adherence to the principles of the Six Step Process will see you through this Valley of Death. Remember, the best people will support you. It is to them that you owe your effort, loyalty and commitment.

Getting What You Measure

There is another characteristic of human nature to understand—*you will get what you measure and little else*. Define goals and measure performance.

Regardless of stated objectives, individuals will generally do only the things that generate a bonus. Therefore, align individual goals with organizational objectives—and then measure those factors that indicate progress.

As a managing partner, I kept three reports on my desk—lists of unbilled work, uncollected billings and new business targets. No conversation was concluded without my asking, "How we doin' on collecting the Ace Tool receivable?" or "Why haven't we billed the Global work yet?" or "When are we meeting with the CEO of Hot Prospect Inc.?" This constant reinforcement reminded everyone that growth and cash flow were their responsibility—and they would be held accountable for their performance. It proved very effective. You *will* get what you measure.

A similar approach works with troubled companies. Among the first things I do is prominently display progress toward achieving stated goals— monthly sales, inventory reduction, cash collections or geographic consolidation. In doing so, you focus attention and reinforce your insistence on results. And you create the victories that sustain continued success. You will see results. And that provides the opportunity to offer praise and encouragement.

When you align strategic objectives with the criteria that reward individual performance, you link organizational excellence with the behavior that will achieve and sustain it.

It's not just results that should be measured. Also measure compliance with the process that produced them. I grew up in a culture that said, "We don't care how you do it—just make the numbers." Such cultures rarely achieve excellence, because they underinvest in people, products and quality.

Our attitude changed when we decided that compliance with the *process* for producing a quality product, desired behavior or financial results was as important as the results themselves. For example, unless we complied with our quality control process, the fact that no errors emerged in our work did not mean they weren't there. Measuring results—and compliance with the process that produced them—soon aligned our performance with our strategic objectives.

Define your strategic objectives, align them with the criteria for reward—and then measure compliance.

Achieve a Competitive Advantage

Organizations are fundamentally the same. There are never enough quality people, cash or vital material. Customers are demanding. Ever increasing demands for technology are killing you.

In this environment, how do you differentiate your company?

There is a story about two guys walking through the woods and coming upon a mean ole smelly, nasty bear. As one guy turns to run, the other straps on his sneakers.

"What are you doing?" asks his buddy. "You can't outrun that bear."

"No," responds his friend, "But I can outrun you."

That bear is the marketplace and the two guys are competitors. And the bear is going to eat one of them—most likely the laggard.

Which one are you?

Are you the business as usual guy strolling along and *hoping* you won't get eaten, or the smart guy lacing on your Six Step Process sneakers to *ensure* you don't get eaten?

The good news is the inherent inertia of your competitors. The mere act of initiating the Six Step Process is a differentiator. It may not last forever—in fact, assume it won't. But the quicker you begin and the better you execute, the greater will be your competitive advantage. And the better you will respond when that other team decides to strap on their own sneakers.

More likely, the other team has *already* strapped them on—and is rapidly pulling away.

So you had better get going.

CHECKPOINTS on the Road to Heaven

Review the change process—Step One of the Six Step Process—by answering these questions:

What is the primary form of motivation in your organization?

- Fear of failure, criticism, company failure, loss of jobs?

- Greed—an overwhelming focus on short-term results? Competition for a larger bonus, more options? Unrelenting focus on stock price, above anything else?

- Pride? We just want to be the best—and we know we are, because we try to improve every day. We are all in it together. We just will not tolerate being anything other than the best.

Individuals are motivated fundamentally by self-interest, but once their fears and insecurities have been addressed, they will respond with pride to the challenge of pursuing excellence. Pride is the ultimate motivator of the best people in pursuit of excellence.

It is human nature to resist change. This resistance will be manifested in five emotions—denial, fear, anger, resignation, triumph. Experiencing them is akin to traversing the Valley of Death.

- *Denial.* This too shall pass. Just ignore it.

- *Fear.* They really expect us to do *that* in addition to everything else?

- *Anger.* Resistance—both active and passive—is directed at you and your change initiative.

- *Resignation.* Your leadership—and commitment to positive change—generates support from the best in your organization.

- *Triumph.* Momentum builds in response to your active leadership.

The key to traversing the Valley of Death is trust. Trust is created in a values-based community, through skilled and sensitive leadership.

You will get what you measure. Align the personal goals of your people with the strategic objectives of your organization. Then measure compliance, because you will only get what you measure.

Implementation of the Six Step Process gives your firm a competitive advantage. Organizations basically face the same challenges—and are equally reluctant to face them. The sooner you begin and the more diligent your implementation, the greater your advantage. Also assume the opposite—that your competitors *will* eventually begin the march to Heaven.

So you had better get started.

You now understand the fundamentals of motivation, human reaction to change, the challenges of the Valley of Death, the importance of measurement and the opportunity for differentiation. This puts you in a good position to move to Step Two on the road to Heaven—creating an environment of trust, in which individual members are motivated to achieve excellence.

Step Two

Build a
Values-Based Community

Integrity is at the heart of a values-based community.

How would you define a community?

Fundamentally, it is a group of individuals who come together to achieve common, mutually agreed-upon objectives. Communities have been the foundation of human interaction since our ancestors learned to live in the same cave. The basic form of community is a family. Over time, families evolved into neighborhoods and eventually into countries, religions, universities and similar institutions, each with their own standards of admission, beliefs and codes of acceptable behavior. These commonly held standards, rules and values are referred to as *culture*. As a culture is passed from generation to generation, it becomes "the way we do it around here."

Communities that demand excellence survive and prosper. Those that tolerate mediocrity do not.

Great institutions maintain high standards. The keepers of those cultures know that perpetuating high standards is essential for survival. Your organization is a community. Its future depends upon the substance of its culture.

Excellence begins with high standards of admission. Spartan mothers sent their sons to battle with the admonishment to come back "with your shield or on it." Young Native Americans were admitted to the society of warriors only after completing a demanding physical and psychological rite of passage. Religious institutions have long subjected their priests, rabbis and monks to years of intense education before accepting them into the community of their peers.

Among my proudest moments was being commissioned a Marine officer. I gladly paid the high price of admission. I also recall my pride in being admitted to the partnership of my firm—the culmination of nine hard, demanding years of work and study.

Membership in communities of excellence generates the individual pride needed to sustain them.

Think about the select groups to which you were admitted. Do you recall how proud you were to join your fraternity, sorority or favorite club? Or strutting around campus in your shiny new letter jacket? Remember reading that letter of admission to the college of your choice? What were your feelings after passing the bar, CPA, real estate or brokerage exam? Do you recall being recognized as a member of the Million Dollar Sales Club?

It was a joyous occasion. You had earned the right to membership in an elite group and deserved to be proud of your accomplishment.

Being a member of a community of excellence carries with it obligations as well as privileges. Try skipping practice a few times and see whether your teammates let you wear your letter jacket. Run your ship aground and find out how long the Navy lets you remain its captain. I can recall the principal of my high school telling us that unless our public behavior reflected the school's values, our letter jackets would hang in his closet, not ours.

If admission to a community means accepting its cultural mores, then rejection constitutes unilateral resignation. Adherence to the culture is required for continued membership. Benedict Arnold's picture is not among those of the Revolutionary War generals hanging at West Point.

Core Values—The Foundation of the Community

Values are the foundation of all communities, including your organization. They are the fundamental rules—stated or unstated—that define behavior. They are generally accepted and willingly followed. These values may contribute positively to long-term excellence or inhibit it.

Irrespective, don't confuse them with a corporate value statement list of feel-good, politically correct slogans slapped together by some committee, inscribed on Lucite wall plaques, hung on the lobby wall and quickly forgotten.

What are the core values of your organization—those that dictate behavior? To find out, answer these questions:

- Forget the plaque in the lobby, how does the place really work?

- What behavior is considered acceptable?

- What are the characteristics of leadership?

- Which practices are rewarded?

- Which are condoned?

- What are the real "do it or else" standards?

- Does your organization reward outstanding performers, compared with those who do just enough to look good?

- How does it foster mutual respect and true teamwork?

- Are leaders held accountable for their actions and decisions? In short, do they walk the talk? For that matter, have they even bothered to articulate the values the organization stands for and to which it is committed?

Now review your answers. Do you like what you see? Will your values facilitate the pursuit of excellence? If not, then what are the core values that will drive organizational excellence?

Remember the definition of *core*. These values must be shared, easily understood and universally accepted. Everybody lives by them. You are—organizationally and individually—going to "walk the talk" from the boardroom to the shipping dock. These values will be the benchmarks against which decisions will be made, behavior evaluated and individuals measured and rewarded.

Organizations of excellence generally include these core values:

- Highly value people
- Quality service to clients
- Fair treatment for people
- Respect for diversity
- Strong business ethics
- Cooperating collegially to solve problems
- Fostering trust with our stakeholders
- Accountability

- Respect for hard work
- Character
- Corporate citizenship
- Respect for the environment
- Adopting best practices
- Adherence to high standards of professionalism
- Listening to our people and customers
- Seeking continuous improvement
- Honesty in dealings with others

That is an excellent list of positive attributes. Most organizations would be well served if these values reflected the way the place worked.

Now reduce your list to those that are truly *core*. Which would you remove?

Which are crucial?

Group values into categories or themes, then name them.

When you complete this exercise, in all likelihood, you will be reduced to four: *Integrity, Teamwork, Respect* and *Responsibility*.

Now test their validity:

- Which would you delete?
- How about integrity?
- Can you succeed without teamwork?
- Do you wish to be in a culture where respect is not important?
- Is success possible without responsibility?

- Can you live with these?
- Do you want to live without them?

If you would delete none of them, they must be *core.* Since you are going to live with them, it's important that you understand what they mean.

Integrity

Personal and institutional integrity are the heart of a values-based community.

Do you consider yourself to be a person of intelligence and integrity?

What does it mean to *act* with integrity? It is certainly more than not cheating on your spouse or expense report, though they count too. The foundation of integrity is *intellectual honesty*—standing for the truth in everything you say and do. What is the truth? If you can't picture explaining your actions to your family, then you know the answer.

Your opinions, arguments and decisions must be based on facts and logic. They are not ill-founded, emotional, self-centered or politically motivated. Deception—for any reason—is unacceptable. For instance, intellectual honesty precludes your talking a subordinate into sticking around for an unlikely promotion. It also precludes your taking credit for the work or ideas of a colleague.

Rationalization as a basis for decision-making is the antithesis of intellectual honesty. "We need to do this in the best interests of the business" usually means making a decision that defies logic, but is consistent with someone's political agenda. Such decisions are fatal to the organization—and every time one is made, an innocent party is damaged.

At the time of our merger, a very competent managing partner was replaced by a person whose primary qualification was, in my opinion, membership in one of the Firm's politically influential constituencies. The appointment was celebrated for advancing this individual's career. What about the other partner's career? What about the staff and clients in that office, who were now deprived of capable leadership? I have always refused to make such decisions. When pressured, I would ask, "When selecting a brain surgeon, would you pick the best or the politically correct choice?"

How often have you heard that perception is reality? How intellectually honest is it to make decisions on the basis of superficial impressions?

What if you are wrong?

Among the smart, honest friends I have been fortunate to accumulate is a Ph.D. in Industrial Psychology, an author, academic and the founder of two very successful software firms. My friend is a Westerner to the core—complete with the garb, drawl, irreverent personality and outspoken commitment to the truth and to those who speak it. He is equally comfortable in a trout stream, boardroom or classroom. In other words, he's a great person, friend and mentor. He's also the stereotype of an Easterner's perception of a Westerner.

My colleagues resisted my proposal to buy his company. In spite of the evidence, my friend was not *perceived* as smart enough to develop sophisticated software. Well, he's smart enough to buy and sell most of us. Because of perception, we missed an opportunity to acquire a valuable asset.

Be careful of leaping to conclusions. Perception is not always reality. Intellectual honesty and good business require that you determine the difference before acting.

Procrastination is being intellectually dishonest. Situations only worsen. When the flames become a raging fire, the ramifications can only be averse to the best interests of your company. And while you dither, your people will be forced to make the decisions—instead of you. Causing others to assume your responsibilities—and your risk—is not being intellectually honest.

Integrity encompasses *moral courage.*

Moral courage requires speaking when you know you must. I've sat in countless meetings listening to people talk around obvious but politically sensitive issues, hoping someone would speak up. Finally, this task would fall to me—along with the heat. Later, my colleagues would help salve my wounds by telling me how much they admired me.

Moral courage also requires supporting a colleague who is not getting deserved credit or who is being criticized for opinions with which you agree. Staring at the ceiling while someone is being mistreated is not being morally courageous. Moral courage requires making the difficult decisions—and then acting on them. It means persevering in the face of resistance and adversity because you know you *must.*

Integrity is the most *core* of core values, because it is the foundation for all others.

Teamwork

Teamwork is the process of people working together toward a common goal. Teamwork, and the process by which it is created, is a characteristic of a values-based community.

Teamwork leverages the skills of individuals. Collaboration with others is inevitably required to accomplish difficult tasks. The complementary skills of team members accelerate the problem-solving process. Being part of a team also satisfies our intrinsic need to belong. For most people, it is a positive, rewarding experience.

Teamwork involves the concept of giving. It means putting the team's interests before your own. You do your share of the work and participate ratably in the results. As a team member, you have the right—and the responsibility—to participate in the decision-making process. It is the essence of teamwork to willingly implement resulting decisions, whether or not you agree with them. That's tough—and contrary to human nature—but it is the only way a team can function.

The basis for effecting teamwork is fairness. As a leader, strive to ensure that all points of view are considered. Counsel those who are having difficulty expressing their views or understanding their obligations.

What do you do when you overhear someone at the water cooler decline to participate in an agreed-upon decision? Do you ignore it? Challenge the person? The answer depends on your moral courage. I suggest that you challenge the person in private. In all likelihood, the water cooler speech was bravado. If not, your best approach is to explore the individual's reasons and suggest that these reservations be discussed with the team leader. Talking to the team leader yourself is a last resort—and only to be done with both people's knowledge—or better, with them in hand.

Teamwork is a powerful force in achieving organizational excellence. I was on athletic teams from Little League through college. But my most memorable team-building experience came as a young Marine officer responsible for forming a platoon. Over a long summer of training, hard work and teaching, my sergeants and I created an effective team of young men fresh from boot camp and a few veterans, including several from the brig who welcomed a second chance. Creating a team characterized by technical competence, respect, loyalty and commitment to excellence—and then leading it in harm's way—has been among my most beneficial experiences.

I saw the power of teamwork several summers ago, when I came down with an attack of Hepatitis A. It was debilitating and I was flat on my back. The following six weeks were an active period of budget preparation and forward-year planning, all while monitoring our global organization. Though I was only superficially involved, my team performed as if nothing was amiss.

Their performance resulted from *years* of effective, consistent team-building.

Respect

Respect is the basis for the teamwork needed to create a values-based community. It binds you to your staff and to this community. It binds your company to its customers, suppliers, shareholders, government agencies and even its competition. They all deserve to be treated with respect. And respect is required to ensure their cooperation.

The foundation of respect is common courtesy. When in doubt, try the Golden Rule. Keep your emotions in check. Return phone calls and e-mails promptly, show up on time for meetings prepared to participate and listen to others' points of view. Be tactful, but do not confuse listening with agreeing. There is a difference.

Praise in public, critique in private. Nothing is to be served by embarrassing someone in public. Such a lack of respect will undermine your future relationship and contribute nothing to solving the problem. If confronted in public, suggest that this conversation be conducted privately. By demanding respect, you demonstrate its importance.

Communities of excellence respect diversity.

Make decisions, consider opinions and treat, promote, reward and terminate individuals without regard to race, color, gender, creed or national origin. Everyone is entitled to an opinion and an equal right to succeed or fail. Though you are not obligated to agree with all points of view, demonstrate respect for those expressing them.

Take care in discussing diversity, because few issues will stoke emotional fires like diversity. I have had my share of stress over it—some I deserved, some I did not.

One afternoon, as I completed the standard welcome aboard speech to new staff hires, a young woman approached me. She said, "I could not help noting that you used 'he' about thirty times in your comments, but 'she' only about ten. Is that what I can expect around here?" I suggested that before reaching a conclusion, she should speak with any of the many women in the office, including partners and staff. If she was still concerned after speaking with them, she should come to see me. I was pleased to see she soon realized that in our office, respect meant equal opportunity and deeds counted far more than impolitic words.

Respect means being scrupulously fair, but not intimidated by vocal constituencies who see disagreement as not respecting them or their issues. Respect for diversity does not entail special treatment for special interest groups. Diversity is an important objective for any values-based community—but it is not *the* objective.

As the new managing partner of a large office, I was presented with a proposed Work/Life policy statement. Unfortunately, it provided a virtual blank check to one constituency—single mothers. I returned it with the assurance that I would support any policy—provided it met two nonnegotiable criteria. First, it must in no way compromise client service. Second, everyone in the office, regardless of his or her personal circumstances, must consider it fair.

My experience as a managing partner had taught me that for every single mother, there is a father with an alcoholic wife, or a woman providing care to an elderly parent, or a parent dealing with a troubled or ill child. Respect and intellectual honesty require that you respond to the legitimate needs of every constituency, not just those with a vocal, politically acceptable point of view.

After about ninety days of castigating me for my lack of respect and for being against everything from women in general to motherhood and children in particular, my colleagues relented. They then drafted an excellent, comprehensive Work/Life policy that became the firm standard.

Listening does not mean agreement, and lack of agreement does not constitute a lack of respect.

Responsibility

Men and women of integrity assume responsibility for everything they say, do, commit to do, or fail to do. They meet deadlines and do their share of the work. When they make a mistake, they accept responsibility without blame, excuses or whining and commit themselves to rectifying it and learning from the experience. They take pride in their dependability.

The essence of responsibility is self-discipline —not necessarily a popular concept, as it conjures up unpleasant images of stress. But that willingness to accept the pressure of accountability exemplifies those committed to excellence.

Responsibility is related to respect. If you cannot be depended upon to meet your commitments, do your share of the work or take responsibility for your actions, why should others respect you? And if individuals in your corporate community do not value responsibility, how will that community fulfill its obligations to its people, customers and shareholders?

Make sure that deadlines are met, projects completed, meetings start on time and mistakes are acknowledged, fixed and analyzed for lessons to be learned. Honest errors should be tolerated. Obviously, repeated offenses warrant counsel. To foster responsibility, respond unemotionally.

I've been on both sides of this. Early in my career, I awoke one night with the harsh realization that I had made a mistake in a set of financial statements that the Firm had just certified. It was a long night, as I considered the ramifications of my error. It would no doubt go undetected—at least for the foreseeable future. I knew what I must do, yet was concerned about the impact on a career that was feeding my family.

The next morning found me in the partner's office explaining the error. I was relieved at his reaction. "Well," he said, "I'll call the client, while you go fix it—and then we'll discuss what happened." After he was satisfied that I understood why I had made the mistake, he cautioned me to learn from the experience and then forget it.

I have come to recognize the same look of relief on the faces of colleagues who have just been informed of a mistake and realized that fixing it is more important than making it—provided they learned from it.

Mistakes will happen—and it is in the best interests of those involved that corrective action be taken immediately. Encourage your people to alert you to mistakes when they are first detected—

without acrimony or blame. After the crisis has passed and emotion dissipated, there is enough time to critique the problem and counsel accordingly.

Mistakes are but one type of bad news that you as a leader must be willing to hear. If you react negatively to bad news, you will soon find yourself surrounded by those who withhold it. When that happens, your organization will fail. You have a responsibility to create an environment of trust and emotional stability that facilitates the identification and resolution of all issues—no matter how unpleasant.

Communities of excellence are supported by values of substance. Adherence to them is the price for continuous membership. The right to membership ends with the decision to disavow them.

Recently, I was discussing the values-based community with a class of MBA students. At one point, one of my students, with a look of amazement, said, "Integrity, teamwork, respect, responsibility. Those are the same values I teach my kids!" Of course they are. Your family is as much a community as your work group. Both must create a foundation upon which the respective community's goals can be achieved. Adherence to those values will be equally beneficial.

Adherence to Core Values Is Unifying

When merging entities, much is made of understanding and integrating their respective cultures. Endless meetings are held to discuss this. High on the issues list are the cultural *impediments* to the merger.

"Why," I always ask, "do I need to know about the past culture? Change is about the future."

Rather than focusing on cultural differences or obstacles, create a new culture based on commitment to *common* core values.

Some years ago, I was the on the board of a Catholic hospital merging with a Jewish hospital. In spite of mutual intent and good faith, cultural issues were becoming a barrier. Finally someone said, "We are spending all of our time talking about our differences. Why don't we focus on what we have in common?"

We readily agreed that we were all men and women of *integrity*. We were committed to *teamwork*. We all knew and *respected* each other and our respective cultures. And we recognized our *responsibility* to the community to effect this merger. That commitment to common values created the culture of the combined entity, one that continues to thrive.

Do not become immersed in cultural differences. Determine what you have in common and build from there. If you consider that all involved are men and women of intelligence and integrity, you will find that you have more in common than was first apparent.

CHECKPOINTS on the Road to Heaven

Your organization is a community with a unique culture. Only a community based upon a foundation of core values will create the environment of trust required to effect substantive long-term change.

- What behaviors are valued in your organization?
- Do they create trust?
- Do they facilitate excellence?

As we are all people of intelligence and integrity, the questions are: How do such people act? How do they cooperate in a community? Which values provide the standards for behavior?

These four values are core—in some form—to most organizations of excellence:

- *Integrity:* Intellectual honesty and moral courage.

- *Teamwork:* Working together in the best interests of the organization.

- *Respect:* Treating everyone with courtesy and fairness.

- *Responsibility:* Being accountable for actions taken, commitments and mistakes.

Discussing values may cause discomfort. It's generally considered too personal. That's understandable. Yet, core values must be discussed. Without commitment to core values, you will not create the environment of trust required to meet your excellence objectives. In discussing them, you draw a line in the sand with respect to acceptable behavior. Staying on the right side of the line is the price to be paid for membership in a values-based community. You need not apologize for drawing it.

You now understand the role of the values-based community—and the values of integrity, teamwork, respect and responsibility that provide its foundation. Next you must understand the role, principles and practice of the most important element in creating the values-based community—leadership.

Step Three

Lead More Effectively

Leaders of character build organizations of character.

Effective leadership enables individuals to do that which they would find difficult to do on their own. Organizations reflect their leadership. People of character build organizations of character. As a leader, your task is to establish trust. Trust facilitates change.

Character—The Foundation of Leadership

Thanks to a lifetime of riding airplanes, I've done a great deal of reading. The books that were most meaningful to me have been biographies of great men and women and the institutions they served, led, built, defended or saved. Their experiences illustrate the character required to lead.

I once read—and have long forgotten where—a study of the perfect golf swing. The author concluded that the swings of fifty great pros were vastly different—except for the 18 inches before and immediately after their clubs struck the ball. During those 36 inches, their swings were almost identical. After studying the lives of great leaders, I came to a similar conclusion. Character is the common 36 inches of leadership.

   Leaders have character.

   People who have accomplished great things, regardless of their education, nationality, management style, personality or idiosyncrasies, generally share common characteristics. They are men and women of *character*—with the intelligence and vision to define the future, moral courage to defend their vision, communication skills to articulate it and leadership skills to inspire others to realize it.

   Character means standing for the truth in everything you say, do or tolerate. It is the essence of leadership. So said Douglas Southall Freeman, a highly respected biographer of Robert E. Lee, who spent much of his professional life studying the attributes of Lee's extraordinary leadership. He concluded that the most important was character. In his book, *On Leadership*, Freeman defines character as:

> . . .that quality of mind which makes truth telling instinctive rather than strange. Character is the essence of all that a person has done in life and regards as high and exalted. Character is like truth, the substance of the things that a person has forgotten, but the substance of the things that are worth remembering in life. Character is the starting point from which we go on. When I say a person has character, I mean that when you go to that person and say, "What are the facts in this case'" the person will tell you the truth, justly, truly, as wisely as they know, with the minimum of exhibitionism and the maximum of devotion to the common cause. . .[3]

   When I reflect on those who epitomize character, Winston Churchill immediately comes to mind. He was generally considered a warmonger in the

---

[3] Douglas Southall Freeman, *On Leadership* (Newport: Naval War College Press, 1990).

thirties, when he fostered confrontation with Hitler. Ulysses S. Grant had the character to overcome personal failures and defeat Robert E. Lee and his Army of Northern Virginia.

Leaders inspire us with their vision.

Dr. Martin Luther King changed the world with his *dream* of racial harmony. Abraham Lincoln's vision of the restored Union inspired the country in its darkest moments.

Leaders exhibit moral courage.

As a young staff officer, George C. Marshall observed General John Pershing castigating a colleague over a misunderstanding. Persisting in the face of Pershing's annoyance, Marshall risked his career by explaining the situation.[4] Later, as Chief of Staff of the Army, Marshall kept a book in which he wrote the names of bright junior officers. When World War II began, and in the face of strong resistance, he promoted these young officers, including Eisenhower, Bradley and Patton, over others more senior, but less qualified.[5]

Consider Katherine Graham. At an early age and unprepared by experience, she assumed control of *The Washington Post*. Her decisions to publish the Pentagon Papers and to pursue the Watergate story raised the publication to world-class status.[6]

How about Harry Truman? Emerging from the shadow of FDR, he made two difficult decisions—to drop the atom bomb and later relieve Douglas

---

[4]Leonard Mosley, *Marshall: Hero for Our Times* (New York: Hearst Books, 1982), 58-60.

[5] Merle Miller, *Ike the Soldier* (New York: G. P. Putnam's Sons, 1987), 213.

[6] Carol Felsenthal, *Power, Privilege, and the Post* (New York: G.P. Putnam's Sons, 1993), 303, 315.

MacArthur of command in Korea. The first decision ended World War II and the second ended the career of MacArthur, who had forgotten that presidents make foreign policy—not generals. [7]

Margaret Thatcher exemplified the British commitment to principle when she refused to back down from tyranny and sent a task force eight thousand miles to recapture the nonstrategic Falkland Islands. [8]

Consider the men and women who have had an impact on your life—your teachers, coaches and mentors and, of course, your parents. It was their commitment to character that made them role models whom you admire and emulate.

Leadership creates values-based communities and keeps them firmly on the road to the Heaven of Organizational Excellence.

Leadership Can Be Learned

Leadership is highly regarded in most organizations, but rarely taught. Perhaps it is assumed that leaders can only be born. Or that leadership is a function of that ill-defined, human trait called *charisma*. If we cannot teach leadership, then we must *hope* that leaders will emerge when we need them. Leadership is too important to be left to chance.

Leadership can be taught—and it can be learned.

Early one September Saturday morning many years ago, an auditorium at Quantico, Virginia was filled with 200 newly commissioned Marine second

---

[7] David McCullough, *Truman* (New York: Simon & Schuster, 1992), 437, 839-855.

[8] Hugo Young, *Iron Lady* (London: Macmillan London Ltd.,1989), 540.

lieutenants. They constituted a new class at The Basic School—the six-month course that converts new Marine officers into rifle platoon leaders.

Onto the stage stepped the six-foot-four commanding officer of The Basic School. He was a colonel, the epitome of a professional Marine officer. On his chest were rows of ribbons attesting to his bravery and service in World War II and Korea.

The colonel began by congratulating the new officers. He spoke of responsibility, leadership and character and the training that would prepare them to lead. He told them that their major responsibility was the welfare of their men. "The purpose of this training is not to save your life," he continued. "It is to ensure that when you do go, you won't take forty good Marines with you."

He assured them that they *would* lead when the time came. To illustrate the point, he spoke of a lieutenant joining the First Marine Division after Guadalcanal, in the early days of World War II. Awed by the combat veterans under his command, he wondered, "How will I ever lead these men?"

His doubts only grew during the succeeding weeks of training. Would he succeed as a combat leader?

His moment came when he and his platoon were pinned down on a fire-swept beach. It was then that his wide-eyed, veteran platoon sergeant asked, "What do we do now, lieutenant?"

In response, he said, "We're going to get on our feet and you're going to follow me off this beach!" And to a man, they rose and followed him off the beach.

"Gentlemen," said the colonel, "That lieutenant passed his leadership test that day. I know that to be true because I was that lieutenant. And—speaking for all of us who have gone before you—if we did it, you can do it."

I know that story is true, because I was among the young officers in the audience that long ago September morning.

I once told this story to a group of our young managers. As I spoke, I noted their reaction. Some were quivering with excitement. Others were staring with ashen faces. As I concluded, a hush fell over the group. Finally, one person—in a trembling voice—said, "You make it sound like we're in a war."

"Well," I said, "Aren't we?"

I explained that nobody is dying in our war, but that a huge number of mortgages were at risk. And it is your responsibility as a leader to mitigate that risk. Failure is no more an option for you than it is for a leader on the battlefield.

Leaders must learn to win.

The Principles of Leadership

The colonel began my three-year education in leadership and my next thirty years of endeavoring to practice it. I have long concluded that leadership can be learned—provided you understand and practice these principles:

Personify character.

Integrity is the essence of leadership. Without it, you won't establish trust. Intellectual honesty, sound judgment and moral courage are evident traits of character. Integrity and credibility are not selective. You can only lie to or mislead people once. They will never trust you again and your leadership career is over.

Be selfless.

The welfare of your organization and people

are paramount. Selfishness undermines your credibility and trust in your motives.

Show confidence.

Never let them see you worried. Trust your judgment. Take no counsel of your fears. It is never as bad as it seems. Be positive. Look 'em in the eye. The glass is always half full. If you don't believe in yourself, nobody else will.

Praise people.

Applaud and encourage small victories. Send out the "attapersons" whenever possible. Nothing builds pride and motivates like recognition and sincere praise. Those who experience the joy, recognition and confidence of winning small victories will strive to win big ones.

Establish high standards of performance.

Those in your organization will never perform at a pace or standard of performance faster or higher than its leadership. As a leader, you personify organizational standards. Do not tolerate mediocrity, procrastination or lack of commitment. Model the qualities and behavior you expect of others.

Set a positive example of professional decorum.

In a crisis, keep your head, lower your voice and calm your emotions. I am fortunate that over the years, including those in the Marines, I never worked for a screamer. But I have seen them in client situations. They were universal failures, as were their organizations.

An occasional emotional outburst is to be expected, but successful leaders keep their cool. Their decorum has a positive effect on those around them.

Communicate fully and frequently.

Describe your vision, convey ideas and listen to others on your team. Your agreement with their views is not required, but explain why it isn't—especially if you wish their continued participation and support.

I have written to my people on a regular basis. At first, it was a column in the office newsletter, quickly labeled *"the McMemo of the Month."* With the advent of voice and e-mail, I bombarded them with messages.

A Ph. D. student once spent a summer in our office doing research. She was amazed that everyone understood their role in executing our strategy. She also praised morale, "Everyone thinks they're the best in town." "They should," I responded, "I have been telling them that—and how to be even better—on almost a daily basis for thirty-six months."

In new management situations, I meet individually with as many people as possible. Your message and performance set the tone for the entire organization. Your people are anxious to tell you what they think. This provides an opportunity to present your ideas and assess feedback. It establishes your credibility as a listener.

Meet managers and subordinates in their offices, even if it requires travel. When visiting, walk around. Be visible. Talk to people. They want to see the boss. Be approachable. Meet with anybody who will listen. Since I appeared in virtually every training video, I was not surprised to be stopped in the hallway one day by a young staff person who exclaimed, "Hey, you're the guy in the video!" At least I had made an impression.

Write your own material. If you don't care enough to write it, why should they care enough to read it? Even if they do read it, if it doesn't come from you, they'll never believe it. Nothing is more adverse to your credibility than an assistant writing for the boss. Be positive. No matter how dismal a situation, *somebody, somewhere* is doing *something* right. Write about it. Celebrate it. Name names and sing their praises. The rest will get the message. If criticism is warranted, make it broad and impersonal. Explain where *we* must improve.

There is risk in communicating. Your every word will be scrutinized. No matter what you say, someone will be annoyed. You can't please everyone every day, so don't try. Your only alternative is not to communicate at all—and that is worse. Just make sure you tell the truth.

Finally, follow these basic rules of communication:

- Tell people what you are going to do.
- Tell them what you are doing.
- Tell them what you did.
- And constantly tell them why!

Assume responsibility.

Assume responsibility for everything you or your organization does or fails to do. Authority can and must be delegated, but never responsibility. Choose your subordinates carefully.

Be technically proficient.

Never ask others to do what you cannot or will not do yourself. If you don't have the functional skills, you will not command the respect of those who do.

Be self-motivated and competitive.

Maintain a bias for action. Infuse the organization with a sense of urgency. Be professional, but play to win. Do not become comfortable with losing.

Be decisive.

A leader is an expert in problem-solving and decision-making. Your people cannot do their jobs until you do yours. Listen to everyone, but make your own decisions.

Show empathy.

Consider the impact of your decisions upon those who must live with their consequences.

Be respectful.

Treat people with courtesy, honesty and respect, but hold them and yourself to high standards.

Respect need not be *earned*. By virtue of your position, you have it. All you can do is *lose* it—and once lost, it is virtually impossible to recover.

Personify loyalty.

Personify loyalty to colleagues, subordinates and seniors. Neither practice nor tolerate undermining senior leaders. You need not like your leadership personally to follow it. You follow it, because the alternative is anarchy.

Set an example.

Everything you do and say is noted. Make sure it is positive and contributes to creating excellence. If you don't exemplify it, neither will they.

Remember, leadership can be learned. Review the principles of leadership and practice them every day. There will be good days and bad days, but when consistently practiced over time, your people will respond with the effort needed to achieve your goal—organizational excellence.

Leadership: The Human Element

Management involves organizing, planning, goal-setting and monitoring progress. It is important—but not to be confused with leadership, which encompasses and transcends management. Leadership considers the human element. It is the lubricant that mitigates organizational friction. It defines behavior. It motivates. It enables your organization to achieve excellence.

Empowerment

This is one of my favorite buzzwords. In our Firm, empowerment was a code word for " Leave me alone to do what I want to do, when I want to do it, and to the extent I want to do it." Any suggestion of compliance with process was met with cries of "Micro-management" or "Command and control." We were so process averse that we described ourselves as *egocentric entrepreneurs*. In our culture, empowerment meant individual entitlement, regardless of the best interests of the organization. And we wondered why we were having problems!

Empowerment and compliance with process are not mutually exclusive. The culture of a values-based community is extremely empowering. In such an organization, individuals are not only allowed, but encouraged to do virtually anything—provided only that it be consistent with core values and the best interests of their customers, people, community and shareholders. How is that restrictive?

In many companies, it is a common practice to blame others for your problems. Employees lash out in anger, fear and frustration at an impersonal target. They cry, "Why, doesn't *The Company* do something about our lousy sales strategy? Blaming others is an abdication of responsibility. The essence of empowerment is realizing that you are not a powerless victim. If a sales strategy requires fixing—then fix it.

Confrontation

Confrontation is a powerful tool in facilitating change, provided you confront the problems—not the people involved. Often issues are too personal, emotionally charged or politically dangerous to acknowledge. Unfortunately, until the *issues* are faced, the problem won't be solved. Since our sales strategy was the CEO's idea, we'll just continue changing Sales VPs until we get lucky. Unfortunately, the problem is an ineffective sales strategy—not the sales force. Until the real problem is *confronted,* sales will not improve. It takes moral courage to deal with politically sensitive subjects. Be tactful, but confront them.

A strategy to create one international audit process for our Firm was hindered by nationalistic bias. A compromise created *two* audit processes—one for North America and another for the remainder of the world. While this compromise cooled emotions, many of us did not agree with it. International unity required *one* process.

I sought out a well-respected European colleague who soon joined me in *confronting* the issue of a compromise. Our proposal to co-direct an effort to draft a common process was accepted. My colleague then exhibited moral courage by insisting upon objectivity in crafting the final product. He was adamant that the issue to be *confronted* remained the need for one common international process. The resulting International Audit Process was due to his insistence that the *issue* of nationalistic bias be confronted, not the *people* involved.

Virtually all organizations include good people who do not like each other. This is usually a result of past friction, perceived slights or various forms of misunderstanding. Their time is spent settling old scores, rather than working for the good of the organization.

Your role in this situation is to *confront* the problem by calling a truce, bringing both sides to the table for what I call a *meeting of the family*. The objective is to eliminate tension and related underperformance—not deciding who is right. Through conducting many of these sessions, I have found that misunderstandings are quickly resolved and working relationships quickly improved.

The Myth of Consensus

Every business as usual change campaign involves an appeal for *buy-in*. "Thank you for your buy-in," said the CEO of Global Colossal Technologies. "We need everyone's buy-in to the new program." Blah. Blah. Blah. So what's the message—we have a choice? This is not exactly a call to arms. Their asking for buy-in presumes our right to withhold it.

An appeal for buy-in is an abdication of your responsibility as a leader. Of course you deserve support. But you have an obligation to earn it. Your call to arms, articulating your vision of the future and your commitment to change will be the factors that inspire support.

The concept of buy-in assumes that decisions must reflect complete consensus. Forget it. This is a trap that, unless avoided, empowers a vocal, persistent minority to *endlessly* negotiate. The price of consensus is decisions dummied down to the point where they are worthless in creating substantive results. There is a point beyond which compromise is not appropriate. You must determine that point—and then end the discussion.

The need for complete consensus is a myth. You are not obligated to satisfy everyone's concerns before making decisions. You are not here to make everyone happy every day. Your objective is excellence. Not 100 percent personal satisfaction. Strike "buy-in" from your corporate-speak vocabulary.

Withholding support is often a means of demonstrating power. It is the corporate equivalent of "Unless I get to be captain, I'm taking my bat and ball home."

I've seen this behavior exhibited by partners with the biggest clients and sales reps with the largest territories. I once fired a major revenue producer in a company I was running for unprofessional conduct.

Standards of behavior apply to everyone, regardless of how much profit they produce. Petty tyrants perceive themselves as indispensable. *Confront* their behavior. If they persist, give them their bat and ball. You—and the organization—are better off without them.

An excellent example of confronting tyrant behavior occurred some years ago at the Firm. Our culture had historically reflected the influence of individuals we called "Princes." They were senior executives responsible for our largest and most important clients. By tradition, some who had achieved these lofty heights considered themselves immune to rules the rest of us followed. They epitomized the egocentric entrepreneurial spirit that permeated our Firm. Worse, many young people tried to emulate them.

This attitude was especially evident in our largest office where, because of it, performance and profitability had eroded. The march to excellence began when I installed a new values-based leader. The new leader was soon confronted by a very annoyed Prince.

Following the script learned from his predecessors, the Prince reminded him that he was the senior guy on the Global Colossal Technologies account, one that paid the Firm huge fees. He made it clear that he hadn't bought in to the new program and felt no obligation to do so. His unstated message was that, unless he got a pass, he might leave the Firm, thereby jeopardizing the client relationship.

Our new leader responded that Global had been a client for over forty years, during which time, at least eight senior executives had served them, and it was unlikely the account would be lost if he left.

This conversation—and the Prince culture— ended when our young leader suggested that the Prince explain to his wife that he was about to quit the best job he would ever have, because he did not feel obligated to function as part of a team.

That change in culture enabled the office to return to profitability.

The story had a happy ending.

The Prince assumed his rightful role as a leader and is flourishing. As for our values-based leader—he followed the Six Step Process in creating that new culture, which he led for some years thereafter.

Agreeing to join a values-based community constitutes buying in to its core values. It's a one-shot deal, not a continuous event. By the same logic, when you no longer buy in, you will have excluded yourself from the community.

Everyone is on the same program, regardless of who they are, their political connections or how much business they control. The alternative is to tolerate at least two standards of performance—one for those with clout and one for everybody else.

To have two programs is to have no program. And to have no program is anarchy.

A Principled Approach to Making Decisions

As leaders, you—and your management team —are problem-solvers and decision-makers.

Given its importance, relatively few organizations teach decision-making. Like leadership, its development is left to chance. Most books on decision-making relate to negotiation. Their premise often involves some form of deceit, pressure, or surprise— methods effective only once, if at all. This approach —and its impact on your reputation—is not acceptable or necessary.

Over the years, I developed an approach to decision-making consistent with principled leadership. I refer to it as a *principled approach* to decision-making.

Underlying Principles

A book that greatly influenced my thinking on this subject is *Getting to Yes: Negotiating Agreement Without Giving In*, by Roger Fisher and William Ury. While related to negotiation, the principles apply to all forms of decision-making. The authors' premise is that negotiation—or problem-solving—is a team effort of parties who need not be adversarial. Their objective is to determine relative interests—and then reach a mutually acceptable solution. The principles of *Getting to Yes*[9] are:

Separate the people from the problem.
Don't let it become personal. Be hard on the problem, but soft on the people. Remove feelings from an emotional process.

---

[9] Roger Fisher and William Ury, *Getting to Yes: Negotiating Agreement Without Giving In* (New York: Penguin Books, 1986), 15.

Focus on interests, not positions.

Resist the temptation to focus on stated positions, rather than underlying interests. What do you want? Be open regarding your interests. How can the other side respond if they do not know what they are?

Search for options.

Seek alternatives before deciding what to do. Consider and evaluate all alternatives. Look for win-win.

Need for criteria.

Insist that decisions be based on objective criteria, such as market value, expert opinions, prices in comparable transactions, professional standards, customs or law.

The authors' logic is irrefutable. Their commonsense principles are at the foundation of any rational approach to problem-solving—which involves making informed and substantive decisions.

They Are Sound

I recall meeting with an important client who was about to dismiss us. I listened respectfully as he described his very valid reasons. When he finished, I apologized—and then told him my problem.

I had just assumed responsibility for the office. My task was to restore its quality and profitability. I explained that if he fired me, I could hardly demonstrate our improvement to him or to anyone else.

I then proposed a win-win solution. Retain us for one more year. During that time, we would provide him the outstanding service he deserved. In doing so, I could achieve my objective of demonstrating value.

Being a fair man, he agreed.

What could have been a nasty, relationship-ending argument about the quality of our service became a discussion about achieving our respective objectives. That meeting initiated a personal and professional relationship that continues to this day.

More recently, on another assignment, we needed to reduce an inventory of slow-moving stock. The company also had too many vendors. Instead of arguing with vendors about returning inventory, I asked to discuss our relationship. We quickly found that vendor sales executives were only too willing to discuss how they could win more of our business. Our strategy worked. We agreed to a win-win solution. We returned the inventory, reduced the number of vendors and began to partner with the best—all in exchange for consolidating our purchases. And, because of the volume, we received lower prices.

These anecdotes show you the benefits of seeking win-win solutions in difficult situations. In each case, we each obtained what we wanted, while building trust and strengthening relationships.

Principles of Decision-Making

The principled approach to decision-making builds trust. This is especially important when a relationship must survive the issue at hand—including those, for instance, with your spouse, colleagues or important client. *The principled approach works.* Its effectiveness has been demonstrated time and again.

A book that helped formulate my thinking on decision-making is *The West Point Way of Leadership* by Retired Colonel Larry R. Donnithorne.

It impressed me, because the author articulates decision-making within the context of the values-based community. Some years ago, I asked my direct reports if they agreed that we should incorporate the book's concepts into our training. Unknown to me, one of them was an ordained minister who was offended that I would relate principle with the military. After reading the book, though, he said that if he hadn't known the author, he would have thought it was the dean of his divinity school.

The *principled approach* will work for you, provided you understand its principles:[10]

Determine the facts.

In fact-finding, key questions are open ended —usually some form of who, what, when, where, why and how. Keep asking questions until the causal factors—not just the symptoms—have been identified. Examples include:

- Why do you believe what you just said?

- What do you think you will accomplish by treating me so rudely?

- Why do you think your offer is fair?

- How did you arrive at that valuation (conclusion)?

- Upon what facts is your position (recommendation) (accusation) based?

- Why do you recommend this course of action?

- What will our competitors (clients) (staff) do if we take (don't take) this course of action?

---

[10] Colonel Larry R. Donnithorne (Ret.), *The West Point Way of Leadership: From Learning Principled Leadership to Practicing It* (New York: Doubleday, 1993), 65.

- What do the market surveys tell us?

- What caused the problem and what are we doing about it?

- What are the ramifications?

- Where can we find data that will help us understand this problem?

- If you were our competitor, what would you do in our circumstances?

Identify those who will be affected.

A decision must be most advantageous to the largest number of people. Above all, the welfare of your firm transcends the welfare of any individuals involved. Remember my requirement that the office work/life plan be fair to all and not just to a select minority? I knew that far more people would be affected by the policy than had been assumed.

Identify the moral principles involved.

Ethical issues are involved in most decisions. As a person of character, identify them and consider their impact.

Determine alternative courses of action.

Solutions are rarely perfect or obvious. Based upon facts and moral issues, identify alternatives. Evaluate the pros and cons of each.

Always push the numbers. Your evaluation should include calculating the relative economic benefit of each alternative. You may not select the most economically beneficial, but at least know the price of the alternative you selected. Select the best—or *least worse*. Your objective is to make the *right* decision, not the *easy* one.

A dramatic example of selecting the least worse alternative is found in military tactics. When ambushed, the prescribed action is to *assault* the ambush position. That may not seem like such a good idea—until you consider the alternatives. One is to do nothing—just stand there and die. Another is to run— also high risk. The *least worse* is assault. Maybe you'll get lucky. This is akin to deciding whether to charge up the hill and lose a lot of people, or remain at the bottom and lose all of them.

So it is in business. Each alternative has risks and rewards—and all have ramifications. Consider this example. When I assumed responsibility for our Firm's audit practice one July, the development of a new, comprehensive process to serve our clients began. Within a few weeks, it became clear that the new process would substantially improve our quality and effectiveness. The problem was time. Training would not be ready until September. That gave us only three months—prior to the January 1 start of the audit season—to train 5,000 staff and 600 partners, re-plan our work to eliminate waste, reduce staff by 10 percent and redistribute the remainder.

There were two alternatives. Defer implementation for a year, or implement the new process by January 1.

There were arguments in favor of deferral. It would provide time for a more organized implementation of a more enhanced process and reduce stress. It would be more fair to those who would be terminated. And it would be less risky. The arguments went, "Year-end planning is stressful enough" and "Cramming this new approach down our throats could put the Firm's welfare at risk."

There were several arguments in favor of accelerated implementation. The new process was but step one of a substantial change in the way we would provide our services, hire, train and develop our people and manage our business. The process would take several years. We might as well begin the journey now. There were substantial benefits to be derived—this turned out to be about $10 million—and we had an obligation to realize it this year, not next. Staff would more easily find work in the Fall than they would in the Spring. The benefit to those remaining—more substantive work and better compensation—more than justified the reductions.

After appropriate debate, my recommendation to proceed immediately was accepted by our Chairman. The implementation was challenging, but successful. We achieved short-term benefits in excess of $10 million, which set the stage for our success over the next few years. It certainly would have been easier to wait, but the right decision was to move forward, as we did.

Because of the moral issues involved, some decisions become more complex. One afternoon, I was with several of my partners in the office of a large real estate development company. They needed a great deal of professional work—preparing financial projections to support sale of their syndicated real estate projects. It was very good work. They proposed that in return for giving it to us, we would advise our tax clients to invest in their projects.

Our alternatives were to accept their proposal, or reject it.

There were several arguments in favor. The work was extremely profitable. Having them as a client would enhance our reputation. It would give our current and prospective tax clients investment opportunities. In fact, we had lost clients to competitors who accepted this proposal.

There was really only one argument against accepting their proposal—a moral one. In providing tax advisory services, our *product* was professional judgment. And the foundation of judgment is objectivity. How objective would we be if we were in effect accepting a payment for recommending investments to our clients?

We did not accept their proposal. Instead, we suggested a third alternative. We would review their projects. If they met our risk standards, we would make them available with no quid pro quo. They rejected this proposal and we had no further discussions on the matter.

The pressure to make the easier, less stressful, economically attractive decision is usually intense. Identify and evaluate all alternatives. Then select the alternative consistent with your values. The long-term benefit of making the right decision always offsets the loss of any short-term advantage.

Participative Decision-Making

Much has been written about how decisions are made. The one found in many corporate cultures reflects the military experience of many post World War II executives. In this traditional, pyramidal "command and control" culture, the boss lobs a decision down from 30,000 feet and everybody implements it. Many organizations still reflect this approach. Its only real advantage is direction. People know what their boss wants, regardless of whether it makes sense.

At the other end of the decision-making spectrum is the leaderless, self-directed work team. Here, a facilitator ensures that the primary result of decision-making is consensus. Rarely do teams focused on achieving consensus make meaningful decisions.

In my experience, neither method is as effective as *participative* decision-making. It reflects the best of both approaches and avoids the worst. As a decision-maker, you are obligated to seek input, listen to and consider everyone's opinion. Focus groups, surveys and meetings provide additional valuable input. When it all has been considered, you, as the leader, make a decision.

Build consensus over time by explaining the basis for your decisions and why contrary positions were not persuasive. You have the right to make unilateral decisions—even after receiving input—but you would do so only at risk to the integrity of the process. "Command and control" style leadership is generally not appropriate or productive over long periods of time, because your people eventually stop providing input. After all, what is the point?

Consistent with commitment to teamwork, participative decision-making requires that, once decisions are made, they are to be implemented, regardless of individual points of view.

You are a leader, not a facilitator. Make sound decisions and, once made, implement them. When the facts change, or it becomes apparent that a decision was wrong, begin the process again. Be objective. Decide in the best interests of the organization. Participative decision-making is not democratic. It is not a voting process.

There are times when you must act contrary to the input. Consider this example. One of the more controversial practices in professional service organizations is "up or out," whereby individuals either progress or are terminated. In deciding whether to adopt this policy or not, I sought my colleagues' opinions.

The arguments against up or out were: It was unfair to those being pushed out, because individuals develop at different rates. We owed more loyalty to employees who had been with us the longest. It would deprive clients of our most experienced people. Finally, losing our more experienced personnel might impact quality and efficiency.

The arguments in favor were: There was no proven correlation between experience and capability. We had an obligation to provide clients with the best people available. Keeping those in place who were not qualified for promotion was extremely unfair to them, as well as to those stacked behind them. We were hiring better people than those who were not qualified for promotion. We were losing capable individuals who were impatient for an opportunity. Finally, they were the most expensive and resistant to change.

With little support, I decided that we had no choice but to adopt the up or out policy. In spite of early resistance, as the benefits to our clients, staff and firm of promoting smarter, more aggressive people became evident, consensus for this decision developed.

As a leader, you have an obligation to listen to everyone, but you retain the right—and responsibility—to decide.

Call the Question

In a perfect world, everybody would just buy in because they want to. And then they'd all work together willingly to create excellence and live happily ever after. But you know better. It doesn't work that way. So, what do you do? *Assume* their buy-in? *Hope* it will be there? What if it isn't? How long do you wait for it? What happens in the meantime?

The alternative to waiting is calling the question. The longer you wait, the more difficult it becomes, and the greater your risk of failure. By tolerating selective support of rules, you will lose the respect of those who are committed.

Before starting down the road to Heaven, make sure that everyone agrees to the rules. *Confront* the issue. This won't necessarily make you popular—especially with those who would be least likely to embrace the rules. But in the interests of the entire community, it must be done.

What does confronting the rules issue mean? Consider this example:

As a new managing partner, I was introduced to my twenty partners at a private dinner. The group was almost evenly divided between longer-term partners and those who had joined us in a recent merger. The merger had not gone well. Everyone was tense. To make matters worse, they were annoyed at me, personally. They had been promised a "Big Name Partner" and I didn't meet this definition.

The dinner was strained, but cordial. Their un-happiness was barely contained. They could hardly wait to get away, but I cut them off. I told them to take a seat, ordered drinks and cigars and then con-fronted the issue of commitment. I explained the rules—commitment to a values-based community, core values and participative decision-making. After letting them vent, I suggested it was time to call the question. Would they agree to the rules? If not, then I would go back where I came from. If they did, then we, together, would begin the journey to the Heaven of Organizational Excellence.

These were smart, honest people who only wished to be successful. They thought, while I sipped my drink and puffed. After several minutes, I went around the table, giving each partner the choice—in or out? All replied that they were in. Not surprising. After all, nobody else had been willing to take the job. Their only alternative to me was chaos. That was our last buy-in discussion. And it marked the beginning of a very successful march to excellence.

Unfortunately, it's not always that easy. Once, after a frustrating waste of three months, I resigned from a major assignment. The CEO refused to call the question—in spite of considerable evidence that several senior executives were undermining the process. They consistently failed to meet deadlines and attended each meeting with a never-ending list of concerns. "The challenge of change is overwhelming." "It is hurting business." "It is making people anxious." And my favorite, "We don't have time." They were quick to point out flaws in each proposal, yet refused to offer any suggestions of their own. The buy-in issue came up repeatedly.

The CEO's strategy? Business as usual. He was *hoping* that support would just evolve over time.

I suggested that he confront this serious issue. His responses were versions of "They'll come around," "Your confrontational approach is not the only way" and "You must be more patient." We finally agreed that I was no longer adding value. As far as I know, the project was never completed.

I told my CEO client that there are always alternatives to solve any business problem, including this merger. The important question, though, was which option will produce the best results? I have never seen *hoping* work. My former client undoubtedly has learned that you will only achieve results with unity of purpose. And that will not happen until the question about commitment is called.

CHECKPOINTS on the Road to Heaven

Your organization is a community. Organizations are communities with unique cultures, values and mores. In an organization of excellence, people adhere to its values in everything they say and do. Success depends on loyalty to these core values—and the quality of your leaders.

Leadership is the differentiating factor between those organizations that achieve excellence and those that do not. Leadership is essential in building a values-based community.

Leadership can be learned—provided you master the principles of leadership and practice them continuously. Use this guide to develop your leadership skills:

- Conduct yourself with integrity and self-confidence.

- Stand up straight, look everyone in the eye and know what you are talking about.

- When you speak, make sure it's the truth. Your judgment will always be open to question, but your integrity never should be.

- Treat people with courtesy, honesty and respect, but hold them and yourself to high standards.

- Listen to everyone, but make your own decisions.

- Finally, confront problems aggressively, no matter how unpleasant, because the situation won't get any better while you procrastinate.

There is virtually no reason that you cannot enhance your leadership skills. When you do, you will begin to lead your organization to excellence.

Leadership facilitates the resolution of the human conflict inherent in any organization:

- Empower your staff to do what is best for their community, its people, customers and shareholders.

- Use professional confrontation to resolve important issues.

- Realize that seeking complete consensus may be contrary to the best interests of the organization and is not required as a condition of decision-making. Everyone is on the same program, regardless of personal preference.

Follow a principled approach to solving problems and making decisions:

- Consider the facts involved.

- Identify those individuals who will be affected.

- Identify the moral issues involved.

- Identify alternative courses of action available.

- Select the least worse based upon facts and moral issues.

Make decisions that are in the best interests of the most people. Remember that the interests of your organization transcend those of the individuals involved.

Understand and practice participative decision-making.

The time to call the question of commitment is before your journey to Heaven proceeds to the planning stage. It is a common mistake to initiate Step

Four—the planning process—without calling the question. Without a commitment to shared values and participative decision-making, the chances of failure substantially increase. Organizations of excellence will not tolerate the uncommitted. Free of their burden, the best people will take your organization to its potential for excellence.

After covering the first three steps—master change, build a values-based community and lead more effectively—you are ready to move on to Step Four, Create a strategic plan.

Step Four

Create a Strategic Plan

Strategic objectives without a plan to achieve them is a wish list.

You now understand the fundamentals of change, the role of a values-based community and the leadership required to achieve and sustain it. Now you are ready to initiate the planning stage of the Six Step Process.

Strategic planning involves articulating a vision, clarifying your objectives and developing a strategy to realize this vision. Effecting change consists of defining the future—and then achieving it.

Begin with a Vision

Your vision defines what the organization will be. As a leader, it is your description of the future. Vision is usually expressed in terms of marketplace dominance, the development of a breakthrough product, a major transformation in your business or a significant accomplishment. Examples are, "We are going to be expert in serving entrepreneurial companies," "Our widgets will be world class" and "We are going to be an organization of excellence."

Vision could be anything, but it should be simple enough to understand and compelling enough to withstand the challenges of the Valley of Death.

To form—or sharpen—your vision, begin by answering these questions:

- Why does your organization exist?

- What are you doing here?

- What is the potential of your business?

- What should it accomplish?

- What benefit should it provide your people, customers or shareholders?

If your answers do not inspire you to begin the march to Heaven, perhaps you should consider closing your doors.

I first experienced the power of articulating vision many years ago. Faced with the challenge of restoring quality, effectiveness and profitability, I described our future as follows—"We will be dominant in our marketplace within five years!" Given the condition of our business, this was considered bold and implausible. Yet I continued to link the implementation of our strategic plan with future dominance. And with our success, the more possible my vision became. Soon, realizing that vision became our common focus.

It worked. Our dominance in that market continues to this day.

Not many years later, the Chairman of our Firm initiated a strategic reassessment by describing a firm that provided superior benefits to our clients, improved opportunities for our people and enhanced return to the partners. His vision inspired us to create that firm.

The vision inherent in the Six Step Process is organizational excellence. "We will be an organization of excellence."

After articulating that vision, your next task is to develop a strategy and objectives that—when achieved—will realize it.

Evaluate Your Environment

Defining a strategy starts with understanding your environment. What are the *strengths* upon which you can develop a plan? What are the *weaknesses* that will inhibit progress?

Your primary focus must be on what *you* are doing. But evaluate your competition, as well. Their *weaknesses* provide you with opportunities. Their strengths are *threats* to your success. Common knowledge is a fundamental tenet of competition. Assume that your competitors are at least as smart as you are, and plan accordingly. Planning on the assumption that the competition is not astute or informed is a loser.

Of the many planning methods I have seen, the SWOT Analysis[11] stands out as an effective, straightforward, simple means of evaluating your environment.

SWOT is an acronym for Strengths, Weaknesses, Opportunities and Threats. Use it to identify your organization's strong points and weak spots, and the opportunities and problems presented by your competition.

The SWOT Approach begins with asking questions. Use employee surveys, market research and analysis, task forces, focus groups, customer interviews, competitor information or any other useful data to obtain answers:

---

[11]Janet Lowe, *Jack Welch Speaks* (New York: John Wiley & Sons Inc., 1998), 64.

- What are your organization's core competencies?

- In what areas is it better than your competition?

- What business are you in?

- What business should you be in?

- What do employee and customer surveys tell you about your organization's weaknesses?

- What are your competitors doing that erodes your position?

- Where are they providing you with an opportunity?

A SWOT Analysis may involve only internal resources—or consultants, industry experts, customer focus groups or other external resources needed to provide the information required. It can take hours or months, depending upon the complexity of the environment and decisions that must be made. Take sufficient time with a SWOT Analysis, because it will enable you to identify alternatives, set strategic objectives and develop the plans to achieve them.

The SWOT Analysis Illustrated

I have used the SWOT Analysis on many occasions—including in my role as the Chief Operating Officer (COO) of an executive search firm with revenues of $90 million. The organization had rapidly grown through merger and by recruiting senior consultants. Our vision was to be a large international search firm. However, given our instability, it was difficult to understand how this vision could be realized.

Extensive evaluation of our environment identified these strengths, weakness, opportunities and threats:

Strengths

Public ownership. Our company was the only SEC Registrant in the search industry. We could grant stock options to facilitate growth through recruiting.

Financial resources. By virtue of the public offering, we had a very strong balance sheet, with sufficient cash to fund any reasonable strategy.

Human resources. Our personnel included many excellent search consultants—several with national stature. We had depth in several strong industries.

Leadership. We had a nucleus of very competent and ethical senior executives. Our board included excellent outside directors. Internal functional support was excellent. The CEO was a respected industry executive and a highly effective recruiter.

The industry. The search business was strong, with continued growth expected.

Weaknesses

Organizational instability. Several of the recently recruited consultants were extremely self-centered. In addition, the company had acquired a firm of very independent-minded consultants. We were not as much an institution as a collection of sole practitioners.

Culture. Greed was the primary source of motivation. Many of our consultants had guaranteed compensation. Their primary objective was to increase the payout—that portion of fees which inure to each individual consultant. There was little loyalty to the organization. After all, as they constantly reminded me, "We can vote with our feet."

Management. The style had been to "keep everybody happy." There was little consistency and no respect for management. The board had hired me to provide leadership and stability.

Inconsistent earnings. The firm had recently established an international office. I quickly discovered that it was losing almost $1.5 million per month. This loss, and its visibility, depressed share value. Virtually all stock options were valueless, further creating dissension and tension.

Human resource programs. There were few processes in place to attract, train, retain or promote junior level people. It was the warlord culture at its worst. I once asked a group of senior consultants if they would want their children to work for us. They responded with embarrassed silence.

Opportunities

Restructuring and growth. Our core business aggregated $50 to $60 million of profitable revenues. This would provide a platform for growth. We had sufficient executive leadership to downsize, rebuild and lead the company through the Six Step Process.

Selling the Company. Strategic buyers had expressed interest, provided the overseas office issue was resolved.

Human resources. We continued to attract many good consultants who saw an opportunity to practice in a refocused business. The guarantees of many senior consultants would eventually expire. This would enable me to effect change in the months ahead.

Growth. We had developed several new products that would contribute to future growth.

Threats

Continuing losses. Continued overseas losses posed a major threat. If not corrected, this cash drain would be fatal.

Deteriorating quality. Distraction, preoccupation with cultural and profitability issues and consultant turnover resulted in inconsistent client service. The organization lacked stability. We had to create an institution from this group of independent consultants. We needed the Six Step Process.

Loss of revenue. It was probable that many senior consultants would leave, taking clients with them. Several had already left over various issues, ranging from compensation to personal frustration. Other firms were trying to recruit our better people. Continued losses of revenue-producing consultants could destroy the firm.

Insufficient leadership. We did not have enough executives of character to fill our *current* leadership positions. One of our best people became the new managing partner of our overseas office. Several managers were, in effect, nothing more than shop stewards. They were more concerned with representing the interests of their constituents than in leading the Six Step Process.

Competition. Several major search firms were rumored to be preparing Registration Statements, negating our perceived advantage.

As a result of this analysis, with the support of the board, I took the following action :

Restored profitability. I reduced staff and cut costs. Over the next few months, I managed the overseas office issue to a successful resolution. Our operating cash flow was soon positive.

Reorganization. I leveraged the skills of our executive resources by introducing a matrix of practice and geographic leadership.

Confronted the cultural issues. I introduced the concept of core values. I confronted the senior consultant issue with firmness and decisiveness. I would not be intimidated. The CEO and I visited our people, clients and analysts to generate support.

These actions had a positive effect. Though in an atmosphere of continued stress, the business stabilized.

I then presented the board with these alternatives:

Restructure the business as a quasi-franchise. In effect, the company would provide resources to individual consultants for a fee and a share of the profits.

Initiate the Six Step Process. With the overseas issue resolved and our business profitable, we would rebuild the company. We expected that many senior consultants would leave rather than support the changes. It would be challenging, but it could be done.

Sell. While continuing to stabilize, we would seek a strategic buyer.

The board determined that shareholders would be better served by selling the company. A strategic buyer soon appeared, and the sale was closed on a satisfactory basis.

A SWOT Analysis helps sort out issues and initiate planning. It enables you to identify available alternatives. In this example, our best alternative was to sell the company. Had we selected the second option, implementing the Six Step Process, our next steps would have been developing a strategy and defining objectives.

Define Strategic Objectives

Vision defines *what*. Strategy and the setting of objectives define *how*. Strategic objectives translate vision into action. Without them, your vision is merely a daydream. Strategic objectives are events that must occur, characteristics the organization must assume, or goals that must be achieved to realize the vision.

Defining strategy suggests consultants, flip charts, volumes of strategy books and staffs devoted to development and implementation. It need not be that way. In 1960, President Kennedy articulated his vision of a revitalized America—one equipped to respond to the emerging technological threat of the Soviet Union. To realize it, he defined this strategic objective: *"Within the decade, we are going to place a man on the moon and bring him safely home. . . ."*

How complicated was that?

Begin with simplicity. You can always make it more complicated later. I have rarely had a strategic plan that went beyond a few pages. At our first meeting, a colleague and I drew the outline of our new audit strategy on the back of a menu in a Manhattan restaurant. There is usually an inverse correlation between complexity and substance.

Your vision is to be an organization of excellence.

How will you realize that vision? What is your strategy? And what are the objectives of that strategy?

The best organizations are inherently excellent. Your strategy for realizing excellence is to become the *best in your business*. And to do that, you must maximize the *value* that your organization provides.

Being the best is the only strategy that will achieve excellence. What is the alternative to being the best? Being mediocre? I can just see the banners flying with "We strive for mediocrity" or "We want to be just okay." Picture people shouting, "We're Number Two—or maybe Three or Four, but who cares!" That'll get the juices flowing.

The objectives of your strategy—that which must be accomplished to become the best in the business—must be defined in terms of enhancing value. To understand the concept of value, understand the true product of your business.

What Business Are You In?

I remember my first business. I was the owner-manager of a distribution company and had over a hundred customers who demanded that my product be delivered daily, on time and in perfect condition, regardless of weather or my need for a balanced lifestyle. I had a defined sales territory and, in spite of an aggressive competitor, was challenged to grow the business. I had equipment and rolling stock to invest in and maintain. I had to pay for my product.

If I didn't collect my receivables, I didn't make any money.

The business was my paper route and I was twelve years old.

What business are you in?

Your responses might be: We're in the widget business. We're in the information technology business. We haul waste. We're in the insurance business. We sell industrial supplies. We manufacture rocket engines. We're an audit firm. We're a biotechnology provider to the health care industry.

That is the normal reaction to the question. In fact, no matter your unique goods or services, you are in the same business I was in at age twelve—providing *value*. Your unique goods or services are merely its visible manifestation. Value means delivering your product or service while exceeding customer expectations. To become the best, enhance the value you provide. Be sure that you understand the definition of value from your *customer's* perspective.

For example, at our Firm, we had always assumed we were in the *audit* business. Our *product* was a financial report, with our name affixed. By listening to our clients, we realized that we were actually in the *problem-solving* business. The audit was a process by which problems were identified. The product, from our client's perspective, was the value we added in *solving* those problems. That realization dramatically increased our ability to enhance value.

This is not unique to professional services. A recent client viewed its business as selling safety supplies—mostly gloves, boots and safety glasses. The marketplace had difficulty differentiating between gloves, but it understood the importance of protecting employee hands. Leather protects better than cotton. Which do you want your employees wearing?

That company is now selling *safety*—with enhanced value to customers.

Focus strategic planning on *value drivers*, the elements of the business that define the value you provide your customers, and *business processes*, the interrelated policies and practices that support value drivers. Improving value drivers by enhancing the effectiveness of business processes creates excellence.

The Concept of Value Drivers

I have worked with organizations of various sizes in a variety of industries. Each considered itself unique—one that no outsider could possibly understand. Though they have unique characteristics, the fundamental components that *drive value* are universally similar. You need not be a rocket scientist to understand how a rocket science consulting firm would be organized, develop and deliver its services or make money.

There are three primary value drivers common to virtually every organization—people, leadership and the customer base.

Depending on the circumstances, there are other value drivers. They include your asset base—inventories, intellectual property and distribution systems. However, since all depend on people, leadership and the customer base, they are *secondary* value drivers.

People are primary. The primary factor determining the quality of your product or service is people. Their skill, training, morale and commitment determine the quality of your products or services. My client may have been selling gloves, but it was people who sold, delivered and accounted for them. The value of your product or services will never be greater than the quality of your people.

Leaders have impact. Your leadership builds the environment of trust that delivers value. In any business, leaders can behave in one of two ways—either from a position of entitlement, or as guardians of a franchise to be preserved and passed on in better condition than it was found. They must be committed to the long-term welfare of the organization.

Your customers are critical. The financial and intellectual resources derived from your customer base impact value. Every organization has customers—either external to the company, or another internal department.

If your products or services do not meet—or exceed—your customers' definition of value, your business is in very serious trouble. If you are not providing value to your customers, others will.

Focus Planning on Value Drivers

Now look at the results of your SWOT Analysis. It is not a coincidence that they focus on the same value drivers. The actions that must be taken to address your *strengths* and *weaknesses*, the *threats* to your vision and the *opportunities* to realize it involve your people, their leadership and your customer base.

Strategic objectives must be defined in terms of your value drivers. Without quality in these value drivers, there can be no excellence in the organization.

How do you enhance the value of your people, their leadership and your customer base? By being the *employer of choice to the best people* and the *firm of choice to the best customers or clients.*

When you achieve these objectives, you will have maximized the value of your business. You will be the best in the business. You will have realized your vision of organizational excellence. You will have reached Heaven.

The key to maximizing value is understanding and improving business processes. .

Understand Business Processes

Organizations consist of interrelated, written and unwritten policies, practices and information —collectively referred to as *business processes.* They constitute the infrastructure of your business.

Operational processes control how products are purchased, manufactured, sold and delivered.

Administrative processes include human resources, payroll, health and welfare, as well as those related to hiring, training and retaining people and leadership development.

Operational and administrative business processes determine the effectiveness of your people, leadership and customer base value drivers.

To ensure optimal efficiency, monitor the functioning of business processes. Otherwise they will become clogged with wasted effort and, just like a clogged artery, cease to function. This won't happen overnight. It's worse. The effectiveness of your processes will atrophy a day at a time. At some point, your organization will no longer be viable.

Won't happen to you? Consider the current condition of companies cited as excellent in the business press over the past ten or fifteen years that are no longer around. I'm sure it never occurred to their CEOs that the viability of their franchise would one day be at risk.

Enhance Business Process Effectiveness

To create value, optimize business process effectiveness throughout the organization.

Begin with understanding your processes. The first rule of forensic auditing is "Follow the money to the source of the crime." The corollary here is "Follow business processes to assess their impact."

Drill down into each major process, identifying all subprocesses, until you understand the entire business process system.

Planning involves examining business processes. Begin with the most significant—those with the broadest perspective—which, when improved, will have the greatest impact upon the effectiveness of your value drivers. To create effective processes and ensure that they continuously function, follow this methodology:

- *Articulate the objective.* Why is this process required? What does it accomplish or control?

- *Define the process.* Challenge assumptions. Eliminate nonvalue-adding functions. Add any missing functions. Rebuild. Document each element of the process. Ensure alignment.

- *Teach the process.* Insure that everyone understands the process and their role in its functionality.

- *Effectively execute.* Plan for timely, comprehensive implementation.

- *Monitor compliance.* You will get what you measure.

- *Take corrective action.* Determine the cause of any errors. Improve or change definition, reinforce training or take other action required.

The building of our Firm's Client Service Process is an example of how to rebuild a fundamental business process. The principles are universally applicable.

The situation. Our motivation for change was the need to redefine our product and deliver it in a more cost-effective manner. Our margins had not kept pace with rapid revenue growth. The market had begun to view traditional audit services as a commodity. In spite of our efforts, the Big Six were generally perceived as *good* but not *different.* The cost of declining quality was rapidly increasing—in terms of litigation and insurance expenses, client turnover and our inability to retain quality staff. Something had to be done.

For years, clients had dismissed our reporting of weaknesses in accounting control systems as non-value-added. Growth in span and the complexity of technology convinced us that process control was an emerging issue. Increased incidences of failure in corporate controls—and related termination of CEOs—soon confirmed our judgment. Corporate executives sought our expertise to provide *assurance* that their control processes were effective.

From then on, we were in the *assurance* business—identifying and fixing control weaknesses. As the leader, I was now Vice Chairman of Business *Assurance.*

Within this context, we determined that an audit was not a *product*. It was a *process* to gather information. Our real product was the cost of effectively solving business problems. The marketplace was receptive to more value-added services. Our challenge was to provide them.

The leadership of the partner—our most experienced executive—was a primary value driver. We noted a direct correlation between active, timely partner involvement and quality. Our studies showed that about 80 percent of partner time was spent *after* the balance sheet date—virtually too late to provide effective supervision. Surprisingly, overall quality—if not profitability—was uniformly quite high, due to partner skill and dedication. In effect, quality was reviewed in—although at such a late stage—that it was often not cost-effective.

Drilling further, we discovered that delegation exacerbated the problem. Our senior staff had assumed responsibility for planning and client contact. We had abdicated responsibility for training and policy determination to Human Resources and practice development to Marketing. Finally, because we were not sufficiently involved, we were often reluctant to meet with our clients. Therefore they controlled the relationship.

Articulate the objective. We made a number of decisions. First, we decided to maximize partner participation. Our objective was, "Take our business back from our staff, support functions and clients." The partner was our most important asset. By virtue of experience, a partner was the one who could best evaluate risk, develop test procedures, interpret results and suggest corrective action—which, of course, we were prepared to provide. We needed to leverage the partner's capability.

Next, we decided to substantially upgrade the quality of another primary value driver—our people. Just being a skilled auditor was no longer sufficient. The new professional must be adept at analyzing and understanding fundamental business processes. We decided that the processes by which we hired, trained and developed our people must be enhanced.

Define the process. We began with the Client Service Process, because it had the greatest impact on our people, leadership and client base value drivers. I charged a group of senior partners with creating a new *Client* Service Process to replace our *Audit* Process. Their instructions were simple. "Forget the past. Define the future. Your task is to develop a comprehensive process by which we can provide broader services to more sophisticated, demanding clients, in a more cost-effective manner."

In a matter of weeks, an entirely new approach was defined.

The Client Service Process recognized three distinct, yet interrelated phases of our service cycle:

Phase I.

Information Gathering, Input and Planning

This phase was substantially rebuilt to better identify problems and risk, and to ensure timely partner participation. Partners were to attest that, prior to beginning the information gathering process of Phase II, the following had been accomplished:

- The client meets our risk and economic retention standards.

- Sufficient meetings were held and tests conducted to identify major areas of risk and significant business issues.

- Best practices and professional pronouncement data bases were consulted as required.

- An appropriate plan has been developed, agreed to by the client and communicated to all involved.

Phase II.
Information, Fact-Finding and Verification

This phase consisted of the traditional information-gathering process. It provided for the execution of the service plan, modified as needed. Partners must attest that the plan, as modified, was completed effectively, in a timely manner.

Phase III.
Information Output and Performance Critique

To emphasize the importance of information analysis and reporting, this phase was substantially redefined. Partners must attest that:

- Deadlines for deliverables have been met.

- Our best practices database has been updated with our findings.

- We reported our findings to the client, with respect to improvements that should be made in business processes. We offered our services to effect them.

- We have obtained feedback as to how our service could improve.

- We have begun the planning process for additional services.

- We have initiated next year's annual Client Service Process.

Over a ninety-day period, The Client Service Process was created and presented to focus groups of partners and staff for their input. It was then pilot-tested, adapted and introduced on a *no local option* basis. This was the first time in our culture that such a declaration had been made. Making it was a message of change.

Teach the process. We then taught our staff and partners the new procedures over a ninety-day period.

Effectively implement. Implementation required re-planning each engagement. If an audit step did not add value, it was eliminated. We found that most nonvalue-added work was performed by junior staff. We asked ourselves, "Why then do we require so many people, if so much of what they do adds so little value?" We were hiring, training and then terminating them after their first audit season. This was not fair and not good business.

My first decision was to reduce our staff by about 10 percent, or about 500 people. Subsequent hiring would then be reduced from 1,300 to about 1,000. We eventually reduced the staff by 20 percent.

Monitor compliance. The process was effectively self-monitoring. It consisted primarily of the partners' contemporaneous attestation that each step in the process was completed accurately and in a timely manner. Periodic internal reviews confirmed compliance. You get what you measure.

Corrective action. Compliance exceptions were reviewed and corrective action taken.

We achieved our implementation objectives. By rebuilding our major business process, we substantially enhanced the capabilities of our major value drivers—our people, our leadership and the value we provided to our clients.

We also demonstrated the power of the Six Step Process. The values-based community was conducive to achieving significant results in a short period of time. Participative decision-making works. We achieved immediate benefits—about $10 million—while positioning for longer-term gains. Finally, it provided the confidence and momentum required to complete the journey to the Heaven of Organizational Excellence.

Following the Six Step Process will do the same for you and your organization.

Planning Considerations

If you are going to be successful, there are aspects of planning that you must understand. First, select a leadership team. Organize to ensure the gathering of information, participation in making decisions and communication. There are pitfalls to avoid. And, to provide confidence and momentum, create incremental wins.

Success Begins with Leadership

Organizing to achieve your strategic objectives begins with selecting a leadership team. Whether you are effecting change from the boardroom or the shipping dock, select subordinate leaders to help you. The right people are the key to everything else.

In most organizations, there are three types of people. The best are "A" players. These men and women of intelligence and character are the foundation of excellent organizations. They surround themselves with—and support—only "A" players, because they are committed to achieving excellence. Seek out, nurture, encourage, support and promote these people.

Next are the vast numbers of "B" players. They come in two general categories. The first is the "Transitional B player." Transitionals are generally intelligent people of character who are ineffective due to inexperience, personality, insecurity or poor leadership. With leadership, these people can reach their "A" potential.

Your more difficult challenge relates to the next major category—"Residual B" players. They are usually deficient, to some degree, in intelligence, character or both. They feel challenged by "A" players and, given the chance, will surround themselves with "C" players.

"C" players realize that their survival depends on groveling for the "B" players. They tell them what they want to hear. Every organization has them. They are the long-term survivors who always seem to be there—but nobody can recall what they accomplish. "B" players are dangerous, because they will promote and hire nothing but "Cs."

The one thing "Bs" and "Cs" have in common is a desire to run the "As," whom they view as threats, out of the organization. And when they succeed—which they will, if they are in positions of power—the organization will wallow in mediocrity, until it begins its slow death spiral.

I have usually been successful in placing "A" players in key positions. A number of them have been colleagues for many years. By far the most valuable began as my human resource director many years ago and became my de facto COO, principal counselor and conscience. During the many years we worked together, he made significant contributions to achieving excellence. I would not have been successful without him, nor would have the organization I led. I found comparable executives to lead the technical, communications, product development, international and technology aspects of our business—as well as the geographic positions.

Teams led by "A" players have staying power. When in doubt, a junior "A" player is a better bet than a more experienced, but mediocre "B." Mediocrity in leadership does not instill confidence in your people. Rid your organization of the politically corrupt, the whiners, the lazy, those who have failed in the past and those who insist on continuous discussion of *if you should*—not *how to*—effect change.

In those situations where I was able to select my successor, or when the "As" remained in position after I left, the commitment to excellence continued. In situations where I was succeeded by "Bs" or worse, the organization eventually drifted into mediocrity.

When selecting your leadership team, pick nothing but "A" players, convert the "Bs" and purge the "Cs."

Begin with key roles—those that must be filled with your best leaders. Once you have selected them, be prepared to support them. Remember the Valley of Death? You will know you are entering it when you begin to hear criticism of the leaders you selected. This is a normal reaction to the changes they are implementing. If you do *not* hear that criticism, be concerned that they are *not* exercising leadership.

Support them as long as they are leading within the context of the value system. Attacking leadership is attacking the plan. Those resisting change will watch you closely for any sign of surrender on your part. Stay the course. As organizations reflect their leadership, you cannot expect yours to perform any better than its leadership group. Select carefully—and then back them.

Align Change with Business as Usual

After selecting the leadership, integrate planning and implementation with the inherent business of your organization. In this way, change occurs within the context of business as usual—not as an adjunct. To do anything else or delay this integration causes confusion and delay. It will seriously impact the achievement of your institutional excellence objectives.

I once worked with a client who was trying to integrate two businesses, yet run them as separate entities. Everyone had two jobs—the day-to-day job and a role on integration committees.

Needless to say, even the best people faced two incompatible tasks. You get what you measure. When they returned from an integration meeting, their e-mails all dealt with operational issues. They were running two separate businesses as they attempted to integrate them—and doing neither well. Success was achieved when the integration was aligned with running the business.

The integration of a change initiative and operational management must be done as early as possible. There is significant risk in waiting. As soon as you decide to wait, it begs the question, "Wait for what?" What event must occur that indicates that the time is right? How will you know it when you see it? What happens while you wait? Generally, waiting is fatal. When in doubt, do it. Errors of commission are rarely as fatal as errors of omission.

If your initial alignment decisions are wrong, then change them. The organization must be aligned with the pursuit of your organizational excellence objectives.

The sooner you do it, the better.

Consider Organizational Structure

Getting organized is the time to question previously held structural assumptions. Inertia will usually create an organization characterized by geography and the traditional command and control structure. The National VP at the top oversees a regional and local functional empire. These pyramidal organizations disconnect senior management from customers.

Information comes down the organization in the form of directives, but rarely works its way up as feedback. As those at the top become ever more disconnected, local management begins to do it "their way." Inefficiency and inconsistency inevitably result. These organizations rarely work well across functional lines. It's tough enough to get regional sales directors to talk, let alone get sales and engineering to cooperate.

We suffered from the same problem at the Firm. We were organized traditionally as six geographic regions—each with a senior executive who had substantial power within the respective region. As one of them, I experienced the frustration of my senior management issuing directives, irrespective of factual knowledge. From their perspective, the regional power precluded effective national coordination. It was not an effective organizational model.

The traditional pyramid, vertical, silo organization reflects how *you* go to market, but does not consider your customers' perspective. They generally view themselves as a unique, integrated entity. Not a collection of geographic locations.

As you seek alternatives to the pyramid, consider the merits of matrix management. The matrix facilitates coordination, geographical consistency and local implementation. It enables the organization to provide national focus and resources to local market issues.

The horizontal axis of a matrix may consist of functions, industry groups or product lines. The vertical axis would consist of geographic operating management. A health care consultant in Toledo would report to the regional manager and to the national health care industry manager. A sales manager in Topeka would report to the regional operating manager and to the National VP of Sales. Properly managed, this is an effective means of ensuring local control of national resources. Poorly managed—like anything else, it is chaos.

There are three key elements required to make this work. These elements are also the relative strengths of this structure, compared with the traditional pyramid.

• *Geographic and functional managers report to one person—the CEO or COO.* This facilitates communication, coordination and teamwork.

• *Planning and coordination between the axes is required.* The individual at each intersection is a profit center. This person has two masters. Unless the plan is universally accepted, the individual is doomed to failure.

The national goal of the National VP of Sales is the sum of the regional sales. The goal of each regional manager is the sum of the regional performance, with respect to sales, operations and/or cost control. Therefore, coordination is critical in planning, budgeting and implementation.

- *The matrix facilitates teamwork, principled problem-solving and participative decision-making.* Its two-way organization creates tension, providing an opportunity for the professional confrontation of problems. When conflict arises, it is the responsibility of the appropriate regional and industry leaders to resolve it. If they cannot, it can be referred to the National Leader.

The introduction of the matrix at our Firm was the key to our strategic rebirth. The dominant axis became the national leaders of the audit, tax and consulting lines of business. Within each geographic area, local partners reported first to the national line of business and then to the local geographic leader. Just to complicate it, there was a third axis—national industry teams, to whom each partner also had a reporting relationship. The geographic, line of business and industry leaders all reported to a COO. The matrix forced alignment of the planning, budgeting and monitoring processes.

Leadership must be given the authority to achieve organizational objectives. Pursuant to the matrix, the tax, audit and consulting lines of business became profit centers. Prior to our reorganization, the profit centers—and the power—were geographical. As the leader of the audit line of business, I had the authority to match my responsibility.

Previously, the line of business job had been a staff position, led by the Firm's senior technical audit partner. The job had no operational or financial authority. Accordingly, the policies, procedures and processes "rolled out"—or better yet, "rolled down" —from his office—were inconsistently implemented.

This changed with the introduction of the matrix. I now had the requisite national authority, including the authority to determine compensation. We quickly began to achieve our objectives.

The matrix structure is universally applicable. On a recent assignment, I introduced it to a manufacturing distribution company. We needed to better coordinate the national functions of sales, inventory control, customer service and distribution with local customer service. Functional and geographic managers reported to me. Communication, financial performance and customer service all rapidly improved.

I recommend the matrix to improve communication. The matrix will effect coordination to achieve strategic and operating results across the business— any business. But if you adopt it, make it work!

Planning Pitfalls

Planning is fraught with risks, obstacles and pitfalls. It is easy to become bogged down. You must act. Instill a sense of urgency. Avoid the "Best Practices Trap." Capture the low-hanging fruit, but avoid the snakes in the branches.

Create a sense of urgency. The tendency in any change process is to go slowly. Resist it. There is never enough information. And there never is enough time to get it. You will be constantly pressured to defer the decision pending additional information.

Before doing so, ask these questions: What will more information tell you that you don't already know? And what alternatives will it identify that you don't already have?

When the answer to both is not much, then make a decision. If additional information indicates a new course of action, then so be it.

Waiting for the last 20 percent of information will take longer than gathering the first 80 percent. Waiting means never implementing. Leadership must have a bias for action.

Beware of the best practices trap. Focusing on best practices is another well-publicized management fad. The trap is the inherent implication that there is one great mousetrap that, when built, will enable you to *leapfrog* your competition. All you need do is set about the never-ending task of building it—whatever *it* is.

I recall waiting for our technocrats to build *The All Time Great Best Practices Data Base* that would leapfrog anything in the marketplace. After waiting over a year for this wonder weapon, we built our own and brought it to market in a matter of months.

The merger of two entities presents a typical best practices challenge. Now you have two of everything. How do you decide which is *best*? Identify the criteria to define *best*. Then align them into an overall process. The danger in picking the *best*—whatever that is—of each process or element of a process is lack of integration. Each process element was designed to accomplish a specific task within an overall, coordinated control environment. Selected control processes may *individually* be best, but may not work well when aligned. The facts or circumstances may differ. It is said that a camel is a horse developed by committee. That is what a process composed of best practices may resemble.

Our Firm merged with another firm several years ago. At the time, we each had technology-based audit service processes. Clearly, we did not need both. There was pressure from all sides to run with both systems for two years, while building one world-class process. Forget it. We didn't have two years.

As an alternative, I suggested that senior management of both firms each select a team of technical and client service professionals to evaluate and present one of the following recommendations:

- Go with either as the sole service platform, so flip a coin.

- Go with only one—and here it is.

- Put the two together with the best of each.

- Run parallel for a period, while we build a new process.

Their recommendation, which we accepted, was to use our Client Service Process as the platform, augmented in several ways with theirs. That decision enabled us to create, implement and train our combined 60,000 global professionals in one comprehensive service platform in nine months—well before the alternative of building a new one.

Be careful of seeking best practices without a process for determining *best*.

Go for the low-hanging fruit, but watch out for snakes. About twenty minutes after you initiate a change process, someone on high will start pressing for benefits. Never mind this best in the business stuff, we can't go through all of this without seeing the cost reduction we used to sell this deal in the first place. So, where is it? So much for pride, we're into greed.

Low-hanging fruit refers to benefits that can be captured early in the Six Step Process. The snake is making cost-cutting the overriding objective. There are several excellent reasons why you should pick low-hanging fruit:

- It eliminates the obvious waste that you know exists.

- It sends a message to marginal performers that you are serious.

- It creates quick victories, builds momentum and improves the morale of your best people.

- It will buy the time needed to generate more substantive results.

How do you identify the low fruit? On the basis of economic impact and the probability of achieving results.

Early in a recent assignment, I identified as our number one opportunity reducing slow-moving inventory. From day one, that became our low-fruit priority. The result was a 30 percent decrease in inventory within ninety days—all while executing the broader Six Step Process strategy. Your people know where the fruit is and are chomping at the bit to pick it—let them.

My favorite low fruit is the politically corrupt. Some years ago, upon assuming a new management position, an early decision was to terminate our most egregious example. This individual's contribution had been minimal for years—and everyone knew it. His reaction to my informing him that he would be leaving was contempt.

With a sneer, he accused me of looking for another pelt on my belt. In effect, he was correct. I told him there were others who must go as well, but until I got rid of him, I would not be credible. It was ugly, but he finally went, leaving my credibility intact as I proceeded down the list.

Next to go is your organizational deadwood. You know who they are—the marginal 10 percent at every level who add virtually nothing to the organization but mediocrity. Identifying and cutting them accomplishes your objectives and establishes credibility. Everybody has been wondering why these types have been allowed to hang around. They don't do any work, so there will be no loss. One of the low-fruit, dead woodies I once picked had been running an overnight express business out of our mailroom.

The latest fad sweeping corporate America is force-ranking employees on a bell-shaped curve and then terminating the bottom 10 percent. Although such practices have long characterized excellent organizations—including the ones I have helped create—the practice is being decried as *unfair, cruel* and *arbitrary*. Unfair to whom? The bottom 10 percent? What about the other 90 percent who must do their work and tolerate their mediocrity? Cut them. You get paid to make the right decisions.

Watch out for snakes. Many years ago, one of my mentors said to me, "We could always tell a cost-cutting campaign was over when we fired the mailroom guy." No organization ever cost cut its way to salvation. The objective of the Six Step Process is long-term excellence—not an arbitrary cutting of cost.

Focusing on short-term cost-cutting is another of those traps to be avoided. There is a difference between cutting obvious deadwood and just chopping heads to pay for a change process.

How often have you seen heavy cutting focused on administrative ranks? It takes a great deal of secretarial salary to make a dent and besides, what did they do? Without reducing the workload, all you will accomplish is creating more work for those who remain. Eventually, arbitrary cost-cutting will drive out the best.

So, now that you have fired the worst and driven out the best, who's left?

The snake in the fruit is nonstrategic cost-cutting in response to pressure for near-term results. Adverse morale and loss of organizational integrity are rarely worth the results. Go for the low fruit, but keep an eye on the strategic horizon. And never lose sight of your objective of excellence. In a recent situation, we dramatically reduced headcount in all areas of a business except research and development. In evaluating the relative risks and rewards, our conclusion was that we could not achieve our longer-term strategic objectives by impacting the revenues from future products.

If short-term cost-cutting is inconsistent with achieving long-term objectives, then don't do it.

CHECKPOINTS on the Road to Heaven

Vision defines what the organization will be. It relates to *what*. It is the leader's description of a future state. Strategy and objective-setting relate to *how*. The role of each must be understood.

- What is your vision for your organization?

- Is it simple enough to be understood and compelling enough to survive the Valley of Death?

The ultimate vision for any organization is to become excellent—being the very best at whatever it aspires to. It is the ultimate vision, because everyone can't be the best. It's going to be either you, or a competitor. Remember the two guys and the bear? Not everyone will outrun that marketplace bear. Somebody's going to get eaten. Is it going to be you?

To find out, answer these questions:

- Is your company already the best in the business? Do you meet the test from the perspective of your employees and customers? If so, you are to be commended and can skip the rest of the questions.

- Does your company want to be the best? If so, proceed to the last question.

- Are you prepared to do all that is necessary to become the best in the business—to follow the Six Step Process to the Heaven of Organizational Excellence?

If the answer to the last two questions is yes, then you now must get it done. It's time to strap on those sneakers and start running, leaving the other guy to become a meal for the market bear.

Your next step is to develop a strategy with specific objectives. Perform a SWOT Analysis to evaluate your competitive environment:

- What are the *strengths* upon which you can develop a successful strategy?

- What are the *weaknesses* that may inhibit your success?

- What are the *opportunities* presented by your competitors?

- What *threats* to your success exist?

Your findings will define your strategic alternatives.

Now focus your planning on *value drivers*—the factors that define the value you provide your customers. Every organization has three principal fundamental factors that define value:

- People are primary. They have the most impact upon your quality.

- Your leadership determines the effectiveness of the other value drivers, especially your people. The organization's long-term survival is a function of the skill and character of its leaders.

- Your customer base is the source of revenue and related financial and intellectual benefits.

Continue planning by identifying the *business processes*—interrelated policies, procedures and practices—that support value drivers:

- Identify them.

- Determine their optimal performance.

- Rebuild and realign them to maximize their effectiveness.

Define your strategic objectives in terms of impacting business processes. The key to achieving strategic excellence is improving value drivers by enhancing the effectiveness of business processes.

Complete your plan by reflecting the broader aspects of the planning process:

- *Select a leadership team to realize your vision.* Pick nothing but the best, because your success will be no greater than their capability and character.

- *Align the change process with the daily activity of your business.* Your leadership team is responsible for integrating the change process into the normal activities of the business. They are not separate functions. Do it quickly.

- *Organize for success.* Consider a matrix struc-ture to increase communication between or-ganizational strategy and local implementa-tion.

- *Plan with a sense of urgency.* Build momen-tum.

- *Beware of the best practices trap.* Do not wait for the ultimate solution or weapon. Make incremental progress and build on your suc-cess. Be decisive.

- *Go for the low-hanging fruit, but watch out for snakes.* You cannot cost-cut your way to Heaven, but you can move quickly to rid the organization of obvious waste.

The objective of the Six Step Process is to achieve strategic excellence—not to create change. So hold the balloons, banners, T-shirts and change man-agement seminars. Devote your energy to planning and execution. Through executing your plan, *your or-ganization will change.*

The value of the Six Step Process is in plan exe-cution. This is where your leadership is required, be-cause a plan without implementation, no matter how well it is developed, is merely a wish list.

Let us now focus on the fifth step, execute your plan.

Step Five

Execute Your Plan

1. Value Drivers:
People and Their Leadership

Organizations of excellence create people of excellence.

It is time to execute your plan.

This is where the road to Heaven gets bumpy. Months have been spent in strategy and planning meetings. But now you—or the individuals leading change—must actually *do* something. For many, failure awaits as they begin to execute.

You are not going to fail. You have followed the Six Step Process. You have created the values-based community. Your organization has committed itself to integrity, teamwork, respect and responsibility. You assumed responsibility for leadership. You understand and are committed to principled problem-solving and participative decision-making. You have created the confidence and discipline to succeed. And having done so, you have differentiated yourself from most who venture down this road.

Your success in planning is evident. You have evaluated your environment. You have created a substantive strategic plan that will enhance the effectiveness of the drivers of value—your people, those who lead them and the customer base they serve.

Your execution of this plan will be successful—provided you understand *how* to implement it and have the will to do so. Execute your plan by focusing on your value drivers.

Your People: A Primary Value Driver

Begin with your people and their leadership.

People are a primary value driver. Your organization will not achieve its excellence objectives unless it is the employer of choice to the best people. To do that, enhance the business processes that affect the quality of your people. These processes include hiring, training, developing, evaluation, promotion and retention.

Evaluate your processes by answering these basic questions:

- Are you the employer of choice to the best people?

- How do you know this?

- What do your employee surveys tell you?

The best source of determining how your people feel is to ask them—on a frequent, candid and confidential basis. Once you find out, respond. There is no point hiring the best if you can't keep them. And to keep them, you must develop their skills.

Hire the Best

When it comes to hiring the best, answer these questions:

- Are you hiring the best?

- How do you know this?

- Where do you find them?

- How are people hired in your organization?

- What is the process by which they are identified?

- Who defines the competencies you seek?

- Who defines the characteristics of new employees?

- Do you rely on entry-level or experience-level hiring?

- Who is responsible for hiring—HR or the line organization?

Senior operating leadership must be involved in hiring. But when operating leadership abdicates its responsibility, hiring becomes the responsibility of your human resources staff. This is not a reflection on these unsung heroes. Theirs is a high value, relatively thankless role. They are not suited by training or position to make operational decisions or to be the sole source of contact with high profile prospective hires. It's time to take your business back from staff support functions.

Remember what Willie Sutton said when asked why he robbed banks? "That's where they keep the money." At our Firm, performance results indicated that relatively few schools consistently produced the best accounting graduates. This does not mean that a student from any school cannot be successful. It merely means that in the law of large numbers, they are most likely to come from the relatively few schools identified.

Check your industry. Where do the best engineers, sales and marketing executives, skilled technical or financial people come from? The Big Five accounting firms produce auditors and accountants. My marketing colleagues in graduate school clamored to join Procter & Gamble, because of their reputation for producing outstanding marketing people.

One of my graduate school friends is the CEO of a Fortune 500 consumer products company. Where did they find my friend? Procter & Gamble. General Electric is noted for producing outstanding senior executives. The two CEO candidates who were *not* selected to succeed Jack Welch were quickly hired by Fortune 500 companies.

The software company CEO on whose board I sit recently began hiring, as sales people, young military officers leaving active duty. These highly motivated men and women are rapidly improving the performance of the sales staff. Their commitment to teamwork and achieving excellence is affecting the entire company. Willie was right.

At our Firm, we had always focused on the best schools. Unfortunately, we also focused on about 300 others. Why? Decisions were made locally. Everybody went to school somewhere. Many of our senior people and our clients were graduates of lesser-known, but excellent schools. As a result, we spent an extraordinary amount of money recruiting students who—statistically—did not have the qualifications to succeed.

We modified our hiring processes to focus exclusively on the top programs. Of course, we continued to *welcome* excellent students from elsewhere, but we would no longer *seek* them. Resources were invested in the top schools. We targeted key faculty members. We met with the best students, beginning in their sophomore year.

We also better defined the characteristics of the students we sought. Our previous policy was to hire students with the best grades, regardless of their personality, aptitude or leadership skills. This did not provide the results we desired. There are enough introverted, risk-averse accountants in this world now, why create more? Our evaluations and testing indicated that—in addition to functional business skills —our people required superior intelligence, character, attitude and skills in leadership and communication.

The perception was that young people—especially those with these targeted characteristics— would not tolerate the work ethic of a professional environment. Our annual hiring objective was only a thousand students. Law firms, investment banks and consulting firms seemed to have no trouble finding smart, dedicated professionals. Why couldn't we?

We aggressively sought these people. We appealed to their pride and sense of challenge. Why not work with the best? We were also honest. The profession was hardly a country club, and any attempt to portray it as a workers' paradise was not intellectually honest. Our strategy paid off. We found them. And when we did, we *sold* them. We were soon hiring only those students who met our criteria.

Why should you settle for less?

Provide the Best Training

Now that you are hiring the best people, how would you rate the quality of the training they will receive? Quality training is a primary requirement of the best people. To attract the best, provide superior training.

Conversely, only the best deserve outstanding training. There is little point in investing in expensive programs to train inferior material.

A client recently engaged me to accomplish a number of objectives, including improving cash flow. The apparent problem was uncollected accounts receivable. A staff of collectors had been created to harangue delinquent customers. A large staff of expediters plowed through piles of invoices, purchase orders and shipping documents to supply customers requesting support for payment. In spite of this effort, the problem had worsened and relationships with customers were deteriorating.

After analyzing the problem, we concluded that the client's customer service process was the causal factor. Customer representatives—order-takers—did not understand what information they were to obtain from customers placing orders.

Customers would pay, using their purchase order number—while our records were kept by our invoice number. These inconsistencies made our follow-up of delinquent accounts very difficult. The resulting chaos, criticism and frustration caused high customer representative turnover and low morale. Training for customer representatives was virtually nonexistent. Because customer order-taking was ill-defined, we did not know what to teach.

Appropriate communication and training steps were taken. Within weeks, collections and customer relations improved, while collection and expediter staff costs were greatly reduced. Though it may not be apparent, lack of training lies at the heart of most operational problems.

Answer these questions about your training programs:

- How would you rate the quality of your training?

- Are you *known* for its quality?

- Does it help or hinder recruiting?

- What do your employee surveys tell you about your training?

- How relevant is the training?

- Is it professionally conducted?

- How well does it develop the skills needed to enable employees to do their jobs?

- Are they held accountable for attending and for mastering material?

- Are senior operating executives involved?

If your answers are negative, you have work to do. Hiring the best people only to subject them to substandard training is not cost-effective. They will leave. Quality people expect their training to be world class. If it isn't, they will go elsewhere. The quality of your training is a major contributor to organizational excellence.

One particular accounting firm became especially well known for its superior training. This firm had converted a defunct college into a corporate university. Their commitment to training facilitated recruiting outstanding people. The training also reinforced their strong, quality-focused culture. This strategy ensured that the firm would remain number one on the list of accounting professors—the primary influencers of student employment decisions.

When I considered joining this firm out of graduate school, it billed itself "the Marine Corps of the Accounting Profession." Having spent three years in the real deal, I was cynically skeptical. But, in fairness, there were similarities. Like all excellent institutions, they both used training to expose new members to community values and to convey functional knowledge.

Esprit de corps results from completing an intense rite of passage. Next to combat and team sports, strenuous, substantive training is the ultimate bonding experience. Every Marine goes to boot camp and every member of that firm went to their university. I never met a Marine who did not look back with pride on having made the grade, nor have I ever met a member of that firm who did speak nostalgically of their "boot camp."

For many years, our Firm's new recruits were also subjected to a strenuous, four-week program. This boot camp was held annually on a college campus. Those who attended spoke proudly of its strenuous demands and how much they had learned. Their pride at having completed it—and in the firm that demanded it—had a great deal to do with my decision to join the Firm.

Unfortunately, our pendulum soon swung the other way. It was decided that our boot camp impeded hiring. Students, it was reasoned, would no longer allow themselves to be subjected to such an intense process. Our boot camp was soon replaced by the kinder, gentler version of training then in vogue. It was the Age of Aquarius. *Feeling* good and *doing* good were more important than *being* good.

So, while our competitor was churning warriors out of their program like it was Parris Island, our training degenerated into mediocrity, characterized by sophomoric behavior in Class B hotels. Most of us resisted serving as instructors. Dragging students out of the pool at 2 a.m. who were so hung over in the morning that they could scarcely remain awake was not my idea of training.

As a result, the training was generally regarded as useless and was taught by those who could not create a legitimate excuse to avoid it. The product was no better than the process. Eventually, our training contributed to our quality problems.

In our zeal to become the employer of choice to the best people, we attacked training issues like ravenous wolves. Our first decision was to realign training responsibilities. Our human resource colleagues were only too willing to support operational leaders who were willing to assume responsibility for content.

Next, we examined every aspect of our training and applied corrective action. We asked ourselves the following questions:

- What should be the overall *tone* of training?

- How could it build esprit de corps?

- What should be taught at each level?

- Who should teach this?

- How should it be taught?

- How would training be aligned with other business processes in achieving our best in the business objectives?

- How could it support the values-based community?

I suggest you ask yourself the same questions. The answers are important, because your people will be no better than their training.

Set the Tone

As you practice, so shall you play on game day. The first decisions we made concerned *tone.* Our training objectives were professionalism, intellectual challenge and responsibility—just as in our daily business. We soon relocated our training from Class B hotels to professional training environments, created substantive content and imposed responsibility for mastering it. The schedule was ten-hour days for ten straight days.

Gone were the Toga Parties and beer blasts. The "rules" were explained. If you violated them, you were gone. Asking for *buy-in* was not part of our cultural indoctrination. I don't recall being asked for my buy-in by the Marine DI welcoming us to boot training. He presumed that we wished to be part of the community we were trying to join. The alternative to buy-in was a ticket home. So it was with us.

How did people react to our new, intensive training? They ate it up. From the beginning, the change in attitude was pronounced and positive. The best people thrived on the challenge of learning, supported by state-of-the-art technology. Their creativity and the quality of their participation produced an outstanding learning environment. Their enthusiasm soon caused us to lock them out of the computer facilities at night.

Organizations of excellence instill excellence in their training.

Content:
What to Include and Who Decides

Focus. Your training should focus on culture, core values, leadership skills and functional knowledge. It must be outstanding—excellent in all aspects. In training, as with everything else, you get what you pay for. It is worth every dime spent.

Business processes are interrelated and mutually supportive. Restructuring functional training would not have been productive had we not rebuilt the Client Service Process. Having already defined roles and responsibilities, now we could redefine the skills required to do the job. That gave us something to teach. We were creating alignment.

Team for excellence. To ensure quality of content, we used focus groups and surveys. We asked every group to define the skills needed, both at their level and at the levels they supervised. Their input was incorporated into a comprehensive syllabus of training. Our human resource colleagues created, supported and scheduled training sessions, thereby ensuring quality of presentation. With each member of the team doing what they knew best, our training programs rapidly improved.

Benefits. It took three years to completely introduce this revised program. But the payoff in skills enhancement, morale and commitment to our values was evident almost immediately. Cultural reinforcement is a curriculum objective of most world-class institutions. If it works for them, why couldn't it work for us? At the entry level, people were exposed to our core values—integrity, teamwork, respect and responsibility. At management levels, training progressed to include leadership, principled problem-solving and participative decision-making.

Consider integrating similar training into your career development curriculum. Your objective is excellence. To get there, develop leaders who can take you there. Do it in your own way. But do it.

Provide the Best Instructors

I presented the cultural values and leadership topic at every training session. It was one of the most rewarding aspects of my job. If they couldn't hear about our values from the guy entrusted with them, why should they take them seriously?

Answer these questions:

- Who instructs your people?

- Who are the examples you are presenting as role models?

- Do you know?

- If it isn't you, then who is it?

The logic is obvious—only the best should be allowed to instruct the best.

That was not always the culture at our Firm. All too often, our human resource colleagues were calling on Friday afternoon to find replacements to fill Monday morning teaching assignments. To make it worse, to save money and maintain staff productivity, office managing partners were not sending people to training. Is it any wonder that the quality of our training—and our return—were so low?

That approach defied logic. So we changed it. Remember—you get what you measure. It helped that in our new matrix organization, both the human resource personnel staffing our training sessions and the line management responsible for filling them reported to the same person—me.

You know the rest of the story. Our new policy provided that *only* "A" people would be *allowed* to teach. Teaching—and doing it well—became a criteria for promotion. And supplying the best became a criteria for managing partner bonuses.

We began to monitor attendance. Managing partners knew that it was not good for them when their people did not attend. In this environment, attitudes soon changed. The best people clamored for an opportunity to teach—and to attend. And our organizational leadership ensured that they did.

You *do* get what you measure.

Fairly Evaluate and Promote

Who? Promote only the best. There is a perception that you never have enough good people. What does *enough* mean? In fact, you only need enough to do *essential* work—that which you *choose* to do—and then provide resources for promotion. You simply cannot promote marginal people. Remember. "C" players will drive out "A" players.

Marginal performers. Cull marginal performers, but do so with the respect characteristic of your values-based community. Sensitivity is good business. I remember when our Firm culture encouraged keeping marginal performers around by providing them some shred of hope that they would be promoted. Our rationale was "the needs of the business."

When these people were eventually forced to leave, they were angry at having been taken advantage of for several years. And when the time came for them to go, management wanted them out *now!* As a result, individuals with five or more years of experience were on the street in two weeks. Is it any wonder they were bitter? They could not wait to punish us in the marketplace.

Treating people badly is inconsistent with excellence. If these people were good enough to hire, they are good enough to be treated with respect when they leave. They should be treated as friends of the family for the remainder of their business careers.

Organizations cannot be selectively excellent any more than they can be selectively credible. They either are or they are not. Consistency is key.

Tolerating mediocrity cost us good people who were unwilling to wait for marginal performers either to be promoted—or to leave. The longer we strung along marginal performers, the more the best decided that waiting wasn't worth it. This situation also deprived the Firm—and our best people—from gaining experience on the most challenging engagements. When you fire the absolute worst and run off the best, who is left?

Make the tough calls. As a young manager, I was part of a client service team led by a long-term manager. He was an excellent technician, but lacked the leadership skills of a partner. Nevertheless, the Firm considered him indispensable. He held the senior position for years, during which time virtually no one on the engagement became a partner.

This changed when a new managing partner replaced this individual with younger, high-potential managers. I was fortunate to have benefited from that decision. So have many others. Since then, that engagement has steadily produced capable partners.

This experience taught me the interrelationship of serving good clients, developing good people and their ability to attract good clients. If you can't develop talent from a challenging client and good partner leadership, where are you going to get it? It also convinced me to terminate those who were not qualified for promotion.

This policy may seem callous and short-sighted. You may be thinking, "After all, there are never enough good people. Doesn't everyone deserve a chance? Where's your compassion?" While compelling, keeping marginal performers does not meet the criteria for a "right" decision. Retaining them is unfair to the individual, to clients, to the firm and especially to those coming behind, who need and deserve experience.

Making these difficult decisions will not make you any friends. I once attended a meeting to welcome the new CEO of a large, very troubled company to the community. The President of a major bank began with words of praise. He had barely finished when the CEO looked around the table and basically said, "I have no interest in being part of your community. For weeks, all I have read in the newspapers is criticism over the 10,000 jobs I have eliminated. In all that time, I have not read one word about the 50,000 jobs I saved."

Upon assuming responsibility for an underperforming office, one of my first decisions was to clean house. Of the almost ninety managers in the office, at least thirty had been around for five or more years. They had no reasonable hope for promotion. The only people pleased with my decision to move them out were young people who now had an opportunity to progress. That decision contributed to the regeneration of our office.

As a leader, your objective is the Heaven of Organizational Excellence—not popularity. As you make the journey, you will not always be liked. Do what you must do. Make the difficult decisions.

Excellence is not possible without specific programs to create it. Managers are the backbone of professional services firms. Just as in your business, there are never *enough* good ones. With five to ten years of experience, they are essential to quality service. However, at our Firm, inconsistent commitment to their development precluded a consistent pipeline of qualified partner candidates. Even the best were taking at least two years to become sufficiently capable—*after* becoming partners.

Something had to be done.

We responded by designing *the Senior Manager Program*. Its purpose was to develop partner executive leadership over a three-year period. Those who survived were admitted to the partnership.

Here's how it worked. After two years in grade, every manager was considered for promotion to senior manager. Only those whose eventual promotion to partner was considered probable were accepted. We found the others a job, then terminated them with our thanks.

Over the succeeding three years, these high potential people were groomed. Their client assignments were systematically reassigned to younger managers who needed the experience. Emphasis was placed on developing the leadership, decision-making and marketing skills required of partners. Continued progress was mandatory. By the end of their third year, they were expected to be functioning virtually as partners. If not, they left to make way for those behind them.

The essence of the Senior Manager Program was partner responsibility. Every senior manager had a partner sponsor. Factors contributing to a senior manager's failure—including the sponsoring partner's performance—were scrutinized. Within three years, this program had a profound positive effect upon the quality of our partner candidates.

Leadership development is a characteristic of excellent organizations.

Without well-defined, objective processes for identifying, nurturing, developing and promoting men and women of character, the effort becomes political. Who you know and face time with the boss will be more important than years of substantive achievement. *Looking* good will become more important than *doing* good. Risk-taking and decision-making will be avoided at all costs. In such situations, good people get hurt—as do good organizations.

Remember. "A" players surround themselves only with other "A" players, because they care about the organization. "C" players will run them out, because they fear them. Don't bother hiring the best people if you are going to turn them over to anything other than worthy leaders. All you will accomplish is to drive them out. You show me a department manager who can't keep good people, and I'll show you a big problem—regardless of the big numbers.

Provide the Best Technology

Though the relationship of technology and efficiency is generally understood, this has not always been the case. As a young partner, I listened to senior partners debating our technology strategy. The benefits of technology were not clear. To put the issue in perspective, the profession thought it was in the business of selling *time*. Clients were billed by the hour. Our logic was more hours equals more revenue. If technology cut *hours*, then it would reduce *revenue*.

By this thinking, the computer was a *threat* to profitability. If not controlled, computers would eliminate our waste all the way to the poorhouse. So it was decided that computers could be used only upon the managing partner's approval.

This attitude prevailed. During a tour of the office on my first day as a new managing partner, I came upon a locked room and asked what was inside. After a nervous exchange of glances, as my colleagues scrambled to find a key, they told me it was "The Computer Room." Sure enough. Scattered around the dusty room were several early model computers, which of course no one knew how to operate.

We've all come a long way since then.

No organization of excellence can afford anything less than optimal use of technology. Its use enables your best people to maximize productivity and learning opportunities. It facilitates cost-effective service and improved margins.

You are probably thinking, "Why are you telling me this? The benefits of technology are obvious." I thought so as well, until I undertook a recent client assignment. The company was a $50 million manufacturer. It struggled for years with slim profits, yet had a strong customer base and a sizable backlog of business.

A proposal was on the table to update information systems. But the parent company—my client—had deferred a decision. My assignment was to advise with respect to this proposal. The antiquated, non-integrated information systems readily supported the proposal. Had it not been for employee skill and loyalty, this organization would have dissolved into chaos. Material was stacked, as people awaited supplies that no one could track. Receivables were uncollected, because billing information could not be related to customer orders. Vendors were cutting the company off for lack of payment. Employees were leaving in frustration. In spite of this, it was a viable, potentially profitable business.

My recommendation was either to sell the company or buy the technology required to run it. This story has a happy ending, but just barely. My recommendation was not immediately accepted. In classic Catch 22 logic, my client concluded that this investment was not warranted, until the company improved its profitability. When last seen, my client had relented and the company was finally approaching profitable efficiency.

In excellent organizations, technology drives everything.

One of the best decisions our Firm made was to invest in a technology-based, paperless, audit process. But two years later, we weren't so sure. As it was extremely expensive, the Chairman was taking enormous heat. This product—called the Computerized Audit Process System (CAPS)—was dumped in my lap at about the time we were creating the Client Service Process.

I was told, "Get it fixed—and quick!" With the operating people who provided content, and the technical people who were building it, we evaluated the factors causing delays and cost overruns. We found that shortcuts taken in response to cost-cutting pressure accounted for much of the problem.

I quickly approved a budget—one that would provide for an outstanding product, gave them the necessary human resources and told them to get it done.

With funding and support, they completed the first working version in a matter of months. For the next four years, we continued to invest in CAPS, making it the foundation of the Client Service Process, which is still in use in the post-'98 merged Firm.

The $30 million cost of CAPS proved to be an outstanding investment. However, had we known the price tag, it is unlikely we would have undertaken it. Sometimes you just get lucky. We recovered our investment in less than two years, vastly exceeding any expectation. The benefits to profitability, morale and industry differentiation were enormous. None of our competitors had anything close. And, as far as I know, CAPS remains the industry standard.

With our new-found confidence—and the cash flow generated—we utilized technology to enhance the cost-effectiveness of our client service. We continued to create—and interrelate—enhancements to the Client Service Process.

In less than three years, everything from procedural and best-practice data files, client communication and staff evaluations were integrated into this basic process.

Training was provided with the technology used in client service. It had a major impact upon achieving organizational excellence.

Spare no reasonable expense to utilize technology to interrelate your people, client and procedural value drivers. It often takes courage—and good fortune—to make the right investments. But it must be done. And it must be done right.

The Role of Process

Adherence to process does not make you bureaucratic. It makes you organized. The objective of process is to mitigate risk of error and waste. Develop processes to define how—and the extent to which —individuals are empowered to make decisions. No one individual should be in a position to place the organization at serious risk.

For example, a client that pays a million dollar fee is very significant to the managing partner responsible for a $10 million office. But in a billion dollar business, it is not material—and not worth any risk. Your processes must define how management at each level commits your organization's credibility and capital.

When was the last time you reviewed the volumes of procedures that define life in your organization? You are in for a shock. Your job is to eliminate waste.

Begin with zero-basing these numerous procedures. Most were added in reaction to specific problems, and have been there ever since. All they achieve now is inefficiency. Examine each and, if you can't determine its contribution to excellence, eliminate it.

You *will* get what you measure. Compliance with defined process is *not* subject to local option. Insist upon and monitor compliance.

Procedures are intended to ensure that routine matters are treated consistently across the organization. Nothing is more disruptive, time-consuming or debilitating to morale than inconsistent compliance with process. If you define a procedure—and then do not monitor compliance, that procedure will have no meaning. If a procedure is not worth enforcing, then it obviously does not add value–and it should be eliminated.

But if it does, insist on compliance.

Value Driver: The Best Leadership

An entire chapter has been devoted to understanding the role, principles and practice of leadership. I am not going to repeat this here. However, leadership—of your firm and of your people—is an important value driver. It plays a critical role in creating excellence.

The essence of leadership is protecting the welfare of the organization. Forget excellence. If those who lead your organization are not up to the task, it will ultimately fail. IBM is but one recent example of a troubled entity prospering under new leadership.[12]

Wall Street provides an excellent example of the impact of leadership. The securities industry has never been noted for its long-term view. Consider those old-line names that are no longer around—E. F. Hutton[13] and Drexel[14]—to name but a few. A review

[12] Paul Carroll, *Big Blues: The Unmaking of IBM* (New York: Crown Publishers, Inc., 1993), 349-55.

[13] James Sterngold, *Burning Down the House: How Greed, Deceit, and Bitter Revenge Destroyed E. F. Hutton* (New York: Summit Books, 1990).

[14] Dan G. Stone, *April Fools: An Insider's Account of the Rise and Collapse of Drexel Burnham* (New York: Donald I. Fine, Inc., 1990).

of their demise indicates a pattern in which senior executives forgot that their number one priority was organizational well-being. Greed replaced pride as the motivator.

There are exceptions. Others embed the welfare of the institution in their core values. A comparison of Wall Street firms indicates clearly why some have prospered, while others disappeared. *Excellent leadership is characterized by a commitment to long-term institutional welfare.*

The question then is, if the importance of executive leadership is so obvious, why is so little attention paid to developing it? Much is written about the need for succession planning, but given the success of the executive search business, my experience suggests that this is another area where talk is cheap.

What are your priorities? Long-term excellence, or short-term results?

Do you have a succession plan?

How effective is it?

Execute your strategic plan by enhancing the business processes that maximize the value of your people and those who lead them.

CHECKPOINTS on the Road to Heaven

Excellent organizations invest in their primary value drivers—people and those who lead them. Business processes that maximize the value of your people include hiring, training, promotion and evaluation, technological support and their leadership. Analyze each of these processes for waste and inefficiency—and then rebuild to the extent needed.

Begin with hiring the best. Ask yourself the following questions:

- Are we hiring the best?

- How do we know this?

- What is the process by which they are identified?

- Who defines the characteristics of new employees?

- Who is responsible for hiring—HR or the line organization?

Your training determines the quality of your people. Answer these questions about your training programs:

- How would you rate the quality of your organization's training?

- Does it help or hinder recruiting?

- What do your employee surveys tell you about your training?

- How relevant is the training?

- Is training professionally conducted?

- Does it develop the skills needed to enable employees to do their jobs?

- Are they held accountable for attending and mastering material?

- How are senior operating executives involved?

Align personnel evaluation, promotion and retention policies with your organization's strategic objectives.

Answer these questions:

- What is your policy with respect to maintaining marginal employees?

- Who decides when and how people should be promoted? Terminated?

- What policies are in place to ensure it is done fairly, and with appropriate respect?

- Who owns these people—the organization, or local warlords who demand personal fealty in return for political patronage?

- How are you measuring those factors that most impact the performance of your people?

To insure fairness and consistency, monitor compliance with these policies.

Invest in technology. Too much emphasis is placed on headcount reduction to justify the cost of technology. Its true value is better and more timely information. Technology enables your best people to dramatically enhance organizational value.

Assess your leadership. Is it focused on long-term welfare? If not, replace it before it destroys the organization.

Identify and focus on the value drivers in your business—then evaluate and upgrade the business processes that affect them. Value drivers are interrelated. The best people provide the best service to the best clients, who in turn provide the experience and reputation to enable your organization to add new high quality clients.

2. Value Drivers:
The Best Customers

The only thing you should work harder at than chasing business is taking care of it.

Your customer base—and the products or services you provide—is a primary value driver. Enhance effectiveness by keeping the best customers and culling the marginal ones. Then add nothing but the best customers. Examine the business processes that manage your client base and rebuild them to enhance value.

Look around your organization. Whether it's a mailroom or the Pentagon, few organizations have enough good people. The sales manager clamors for more sales people. Manufacturing can't find enough machine operators. And R&D needs engineers to manage the design backlog.

I was often faced with the demand for more people to serve a great *new* client. Before I understood the Six Step Process, I would drag in off the streets anybody with minimal qualifications. That solves the immediate crisis, but consider the ramifications. You hired, trained and mentored the best people. And then what? You turn them over to virtual strangers walking the streets of corporate America? With all due respect to the exceptions, the odds of finding people better than those you already employ are not very good.

Cull the Marginal

How can you add customers without also adding resources? Examine your customer list, beginning with those you consider most valuable. A client's value is a function of the intellectual and economic capital it adds to your organization. As this contribution becomes *marginal* in terms of the cost of the resources employed, this client should become subject to being culled.

When that *new* client comes in, you are not adding staff to do *this client's* work. You are adding staff to serve the *least attractive* work in the office. Think. Why are you incurring incremental cost to serve inadequate margins? That's not smart.

The same theory applies to manufacturing. Why manufacture and inventory low-margin products? Why burden your engineering staff with non-challenging, low-value design work? If you give them boring work, how will you keep highly trained technicians?

Beware the "filler work" trap. The benefit is usually marginal. The rationale for accepting low-margin customers is to generate incremental profit in slow periods. Be wary of this argument. You can marginally price yourself to the poorhouse. Before you know it, low-margin pricing permeates your sales effort. After all, who can't compete on price? The endgame is choking on low-margin work, to the detriment of your highest margin customers. At times, you may have no choice. But decide carefully.

Customers are not created equal. There is no rule that says that every customer deserves to do business with you. Culling clients may seem counterintuitive to growth—but is, in fact, critical. Try this. Evaluate your customers with respect to:

- Economic value

- Business risk

- Intellectual content

- Difficulty serving

- Any other value-based criteria

You will find correlations. Your low-margin customer tends to be more demanding, creates higher risk and is less loyal. The same logic applies to products and product lines, geographic locations or specific customer orders to fill idle capacity. Economics change over time. Understand the value of your products, services and customers.

Culling clients is especially abhorrent to growth businesses. In the accounting industry, growth meant adding *hours*. Since you get what you measure, we grew hours—taking almost any client that could pay a fee. My successor in an office I once managed—and a good friend—kidded me, "We began to make money when we dumped all those lousy clients you brought in." He wasn't far off.

The litigious climate of the nineties caused us to risk rate our clients. We incurred multimillion-dollar litigation settlements related to engagements with five figure audit fees. While we were at it, we also rated clients on economic return. Clients were placed in one of four categories. The top 20 percent were *crown jewels,* and had to be retained. The second 40 percent were *good* and worth our effort to improve. The third 25 percent were *marginal,* to be improved or culled. The final 15 percent would be *culled* immediately.

Never has the 80–20 rule proven to be so true. Eighty percent of the benefit *does* come from 20 percent of the customers. Our objective had been to mitigate risk from audit failure. But we found enormous benefits in reduced receivables, improved margins and—because we could re-deploy staff to better work—an increase in development, productivity and retention. We were pleased at the surge in morale from partners who did not wish to deal with these clients and from our staff, who would do anything —including quitting—to avoid them.

Culling marginal accounts gave our partners time to focus on crown jewels. The answer to "Why aren't you spending more time on Wonderful Crown Jewel Inc.?" was invariably, "I don't have time, because I'm tied up on High Risk, No Margin Inc.," our worst client. Lack of time was no longer an excuse.

Pruning marginal clients creates unexpected benefits. As a young manager, I was part of a team that gained a large, multihospital health care organization as a client. The margins were lousy. But we rationalized accepting the work, because it would be performed from May to September, traditionally a slow time. It met the definition of filler work.

It turned out to be a problem client. Many long summer evenings and weekends were spent completing this engagement. The client was inefficient and never prepared. Internal control weaknesses necessitated additional work. Their sensitivity to criticism strained the relationship. Since they were unwilling to pay for our extra efforts, the margins were terrible. Knowing I had to work on that client was the worst part of my career—and I was not alone. Office morale suffered.

Finally, we elected to get "fired." We refused to further reduce our fees to keep the work. With summers now available, we moved high-margin work from the peak audit season of January to March. Since we staffed to this peak, this allowed us to reduce our staff. The benefits were substantial—cost reduction to the firm and more challenging work for the staff. We applied this policy firm-wide, with similar results.

Analyze the Rest

Focusing on your crown jewels and culling the worst seems obvious. What about the vast number of your customers in the middle? Analyze each by answering these questions:

- How would you describe your relationship with the customer?

- How are the margins?

- Where are there opportunities for greater revenue?

- Where are there threats to existing revenue?

- Are there any integrity or business risk issues?

- Are you getting a fair return?

- How good is the service you are providing?

- Is it worth more than the amount of money you are receiving?

- Where are there opportunities for growth?
- What about financial stability?

Visit clients. Develop a plan for each. Discuss your concerns. Inquire about business issues. Express your integrity concerns. If you cannot satisfy yourself that the risk is manageable, decide whether their business is worth it. A client CEO once considered hiring one of his friends as a senior financial officer. This friend was an admitted felon. We explained the risk of having such an individual in a position of authority. If he remained, we would resign. We also suggested that the CEO discuss it with his board and outside counsel. He reversed his decision and we maintained the relationship.

If a client is acceptable but the margin is not, then increase your price. Again, if you can't come to an agreement, consider whether your investment in resources is worth it. A good way to determine customer loyalty is to increase prices across the board.

This has always been one of my favorite tactics. You will be surprised at how readily the majority of your customers accept them. A client with whom I am now working recently purchased a company. His first action was to double the rates the new company was charging. Because of the value of the product, he lost relatively little business.

Those customers who do not accept your increases may not be worth keeping. But *you* can decide that and act accordingly.

Be proactive. Know why you choose to do business with each customer. If it is not on your terms, question the relationship. Improve your relationship with every marginal client, resolve any issues on your own terms—or strongly consider culling them.

Review your customer base. Cull marginal customers. Why should the best in the business devote time, money and resources to any but the best customers?

Accept Only the Best

The same logic applies to taking on new clients. Why accept any but the best?

Remember. You will get what you measure. Be careful that your growth strategy does not grow you to insolvency. Back in our growth-at-any-cost era, we were rewarded for bringing in *new* clients. The culture motivated us to ignore current clients in pursuit of the next one. Our process for accepting clients contributed to the problem. Decisions were made locally, resulting in inconsistent quality. Business and economic risks were increasing.

This changed when we decided that the best in the business was only going to serve the best clients. We would accept only those prospects free of defined economic or business risk.

We wanted the world to know of our commitment to quality. *The Wall Street Journal* reviewed risk management in the accounting profession. In an April 25, 1997 article, the *Journal* quoted me saying:

> All the Big Six firms have taken dramatic, aggressive steps to mitigate risk in their client base. . . A sterling reputation matters more to us now. . . So we no longer have certain clients and I'm proud of it. [15]

We defined specific economic, ethical and business risk acceptance criteria. I took the opportunity to disclose the most significant and controversial criteria, and was quoted again in the same article:

---

[15] More Accounting Firms Are Dumping Risky Clients," (*The Wall Street Journal*, April 25, 1997), A2.

> We won't take on a client that has fired its previous accounting firm over an accounting dispute because it indicates greater risk.[16]

When deciding whether or not our Firm would accept a deficient client, the burden of proof was on the sponsoring partner. If approved, a recommendation to accept was forwarded upward, where it would either die along the way or reach my desk. Few reached me. Virtually none was accepted. From my perspective, as a leader of a billion dollar business, no questionable client was worth any risk of litigation.

There were moral aspects of this decision. It is not unheard of for a company to shop the Big Six—playing one off against another—in search of support for questionable accounting. The implied threat to the incumbent firm was obvious. Play ball or get fired. We began to ask ourselves, "Didn't serving a client—where standing on principle could be severely punished—compromise independence?"

I believed then—and still do—that the answer is yes.

We decided that being fired over professional disagreements was a small price to pay for excellence. We also decided that we would no longer accept clients who had fired their auditors, or had been fired by them over a professional dispute.

It followed then that if we were willing to take this position, why shouldn't the other firms? If none of us would take such clients, their only alternative would be to clean up their act. The beneficiaries would be those who rely upon the integrity of our capital markets, who, after all, are the people we are trying to protect.

The New York Times conducted a study to determine which firms were taking these soiled dove

---

[16] Ibid.

clients and reported their findings in a June 1997 article.[17] According to the *Times*, most of them went to non-Big Six firms. One firm defended its policy by saying, "After all, those companies have to have an audit." Maybe so, but the best in the business does not have to conduct it.

When chickens come home to roost, they land hard. A competitor who accepted one client who fired us over an accounting dispute spent millions settling litigation when the company eventually filed Chapter 11.

In the mid-nineties, we culled or were fired by over $30 million of risky and–uneconomical clients. We did not accept any clients who had fired—or who had been fired by—their auditors over accounting issues. Instead, our resources were used to generate about $50 million of new, higher margin, relatively risk-free work, mostly from existing clients. We substantially reduced our risks. By taking this position, we made a statement to our major constituencies—our clients, our people and our Firm that we were an organization committed to excellence.

Unfortunately, the accounting profession lost an opportunity to make a statement about quality. In spite of my urging, none of the other Big Six firms followed our example.

The opportunity still exists. For years, critics of our profession have asserted lack of independence as a primary causal factor in audit failures. Unfortunately, without a shred of published evidence, they continue to attribute it to audit firms providing consulting services. That has never been the problem. The problem is lack of moral courage—on the part of senior firm management—to confront clients.

---

[17] "Why Some Auditors Like the Taste of Leftovers," (*The New York Times*, June 29, 1997), B1.

Big Five executives must commit their firms to excellence. They must decide that their firms will no longer accept as clients those that have dismissed their previous auditors—or been fired by them—over a professional dispute. Until they do, those members of the business community so inclined will continue to adversely influence professional judgment.

In the interests of the credibility of the world's finest capital formation process, those responsible for these great institutions must stop *managing* them and begin *leading* them. Let the Six Step Process guide them in doing so.

Marginal clients, from either an economic or ethical perspective, will not help you achieve the Heaven of Organizational Excellence. Excellence only works with excellence. You must be excellent in *every* aspect of your business. Focus on your best clients, move the marginal up or out—and fire the rest.

Do Not Chase RFPs

Be wary of unsolicited Requests For Proposals (RFPs). Ask yourself what you have done to deserve such an opportunity.

There is an adage in poker that says, "If you don't know who the sucker at the table is, it's *you.*" The corollary in responding to RFPs is, "What does everyone else know that you don't?" Responding to unsolicited RFPs is usually a loser. At best, you are Number Two—a stalking horse for the prospect to use against the incumbent in order to get a fee reduction. At worst, there are fundamental problems that have caused strain in the relationship.

Your criteria for accepting new clients must be stringent. At a minimum, a potential client must be economically stable with reasonable growth prospects, sophisticated enough to be in need of, receptive to and willing to pay for assistance. There should be no integrity issues related to management or ownership. Above all, avoid any prospect that is firing or is being fired by the incumbent over virtually any professional dispute.

Very few customers meet those criteria. And very few of them are found by chasing RFPs. You have not culled marginal clients just to replace them with more of the same.

Grow Your Business

Your customer base is a primary value driver. Culling marginal clients is not enough to enhance its value. No organization of excellence ever cost-cut or culled its way to strategic excellence. The key to long-term excellence is growth. The first, best and most obvious source of growth is by providing more goods or services to existing customers. The second is adding new ones. The thrill may come from chasing new customers, but the money is in serving the ones you have. Your primary focus must be on your existing customer base.

Satisfy Your Customers

The amount of work obtained from your customers is a prime indicator of their satisfaction. I have seen some impressive *client* lists that, in fact, were nothing more than *project* lists. There was little recurring work from the names listed. Merely churning clients does not grow business.

Remember that rule one in the growth business is take care of what you have.

Once you have a client that meets your criteria, make sure you keep it.

Replacing clients is expensive. It requires wandering the hostile, high-cost streets of the marketplace. You are now burdened with marketing, selling, meeting and negotiating costs. Selling cycles are long and disruptive. New work is usually competitive. The margins are thin. Money is better spent improving the quality of your services or products.

Until your quality is consistently excellent, marketing is usually a waste of money.

Find solutions. If you exceed your customers' expectations, you should be their first choice when they have needs. Since you know what they are, be aggressive in suggesting solutions.

It is amazing how often problems are ignored. Rationalizations are, "We've already talked about that problem" or "They don't need our help" or "If I bring in our technology guys, they'll just screw it up and cost me this relationship." These reasons are compelling, until the client mentions the problem to your competitor, who is now solving it. This gets worse. The client is extremely annoyed that you didn't bring it to their attention.

Be proactive. I first learned the value of existing clients when I was a young managing partner. As we improved our quality, we went on a growth tear. Proposals were flying out the door. The thrill of the chase permeated our office. I was sitting in a meeting, reading yet another list of promises we were making to a prospect. We were going to be on-site, providing "frequent, proactive contact with our—fill in the blank—specialists to solve your business problems." Our managing partner was going to personally oversee this work and—to top it all off—we were throwing in a ton of free special services.

The obvious finally hit me. I asked my partners, "Do we provide this level of service to the clients we already have?" The answer, of course, was "No." We were constantly diverting our attention to new opportunities. We made a critical decision that I recommend to you. We decided to re-propose to our clients before somebody else did.

We found many opportunities. For instance, we had always assured prompt delivery of tax returns. Yet the week before the filing date was chaos. The returns were invariably delivered late on the filing date for signing. It was lousy service. Fortunately, other firms generally treated their clients no better. In our re-proposals, we assured clients of delivery at least one month prior to filing. We did it. And it differentiated us.

Re-proposing to a client is like giving a friend an unexpected gift. What's the catch? No catch. You are valuable and we want you to know it. We picked up a ton of work—and solidified our client relationships—out of that program. We also learned a valuable lesson. The only thing you work harder at than getting new clients is serving the ones you have.

Implement processes to ensure periodic review of your customer service. Review their business. Bring in a fresh perspective. Survey them. Meet with them. Ask how you can do better. Understand their issues. Without constant monitoring, as the organization focuses on new business, the service to your existing customers will deteriorate.

Be assertive. The reaction to this initiative may be that you are just trying to sell more services. Of course you are. That's how you make a living. But you are doing so by adding value. What do you say to a dentist who observes the need to replace a cracked filling? "Oh, no, Doc, all you're doing is trying to sell me dental work!" You are a professional. Professionals solve problems. Demonstrate value. Press hard. The results will be win-win.

Be more than a vendor. If a prospect has neither the money nor the sophistication to appreciate your services, then don't bother.

I never understood clients who insisted on a fee reduction because "times are tough and all of our vendors are taking a haircut." A *vendor*? Do they give the same speech to their brain surgeon?

If, in spite of your best efforts, all you are to your customers is just another vendor, cull them, then allocate the resources to those who recognize value and will pay for it.

Easier said than done, you say? Even the cold-blooded world of manufacturing has changed. Before the world wised up, vendors were played off against each other on the basis of price.

Now vendors are partners in the pursuit of cost-effective quality. The era of supply chain *management* has dawned. Cost and waste are the enemies—not the people across the table.

Demonstrate your value. Be factual. But do not be modest.

Develop New Products

Solving problems for clients is an excellent source of new product ideas. From working with our clients to address weaknesses in internal accounting control systems—important, but relatively low-tech work—we learned to apply the same expertise to vastly more complex processes that impacted revenue production, product manufacturing and cost control.

My medical device client is constantly enhancing its products in response to input from its customers. It keeps them on the leading edge of development.

In excellent organizations, the relationship with customers is a primary source of new product ideas. If you can't learn from your customers, from whom are you going to learn?

Grow Your Customer Base

Get your house in order. Clean up your quality. Focus on your customer base. Cull the marginal. Serve the rest. Nurture your stable, loyal, profitable clients. Your customer base is the best source of revenue.

The next best—and necessary to long-term growth—is *growing* the customer base. To do that, target, pursue and win the best companies in your market.

To accomplish this objective, establish business processes, procedures and programs. These processes include organization, motivating, planning, targeting, teaming and persistence. Growing the business requires senior leadership.

Begin with leadership. Revenue growth is among your most important responsibilities. You can appoint key lieutenants to manage sales and marketing, but remember this—you are the senior marketing executive. You are responsible for the revenue machine. If I found a managing partner appointing another partner as marketing director, I knew we had the wrong person in the top job. The same applies to you. Your VP of Sales and Marketing must be in your office strategizing or with you visiting the market every day. Lead the sales and marketing effort, especially with the largest customers. If this is not important to you, it won't be important to your people.

Get organized. Organize business growth consistently with your "go to market" strategy—for instance, by industry or product line. Industry leadership is then responsible for people development, service to the client base *and* the addition of new clients. Since they are interrelated, be organized consistently. Remember your matrix. Your customer needs are local. Organize accordingly.

Overcome resistance. Many people resist selling. They argue that it is outside their comfort zone. Don't buy it. Everybody is selling something to someone every day. It may be to an external market or to another internal department. Everyone must sell themselves and their ideas.

Remember the adage about business being composed of *minders* and *finders?* It implies that sales or account executives can effectively serve an existing customer even if they cannot add new ones or generate new business. *Minders* are order-takers. They are happy to have an order, but reluctant to suggest new products or services to current or potential customers.

I have always found this behavior difficult to tolerate. After all, serving customers and growing the business take the same skill—expertise in problem-solving. What *minders* lack and *finders* possess is enough interest to identify problems and pursue solutions. Those who do neither are not *minders*. They are indifferent. When you hear account executives described as *minders*, check the satisfaction level of their customers.

To tolerate *minders* is to tolerate mediocrity. Creating *finders* is to create excellence. *Finding* new business is a form of confrontation—a scary prospect for some. Personalities being what they are, you need to light the fire. Everyone—not just your sales staff—must sell the company and its products and services. Your business growth strategy must be broad, substantive and all-inclusive. You will maximize results only with a substantive strategy and long-term, consistent execution.

Establish a formal targeting program. If you are not going to rely on unsolicited proposals to identify prospects, where are they going to come from? You must proactively seek them. You know who they are. They are the crown jewels of your competitor. And to win them, you must establish a targeting program.

Targeting works. How often have you heard, "We tried it, but it doesn't work." That's like saying breathing doesn't work. Targeting is not an event. Like breathing, it is a continuous process, inherent in your business.

The key to successful targeting is planning —and consistent execution. Some of our best wins took two to three years of active, organized, continuous pursuit. Targeting is a team effort. Somebody *owns* every target. Everyone has a role. Someone knows the lawyer you need to meet. Another knows the Purchasing VP. Somebody else plays golf with a board member. *Somewhere* in the target organization is *someone* who worked with you *somewhere*. Find them.

Everybody has contacts. At an early Monday morning targeting meeting, I was exasperated at the lack of ideas. Finally I said, "Okay, let's keep it simple. Everybody write down the name of *one* lawyer you can take to lunch next week and a prospect you can inquire about." All but one partner dutifully began to write. I asked him why he wasn't writing. He said, "I don't know any lawyers." One of the other partners then said, "Harry, just write down the name of your divorce lawyer."

Executing your targeting plan is crucial. When I work with clients, I am no longer amazed to hear, "Yes, we have a formal targeting program. Our sales people sit down *every month* and update our progress." Without asking, I can answer the "How much business have you generated?" question. Not much. But what do you expect? What is the message in meeting every month? How much progress or momentum can be generated monthly?

Think about it. Month One: Kick off with balloons and banners. Everyone gets assignments to be completed by the next meeting. Month Two: Since very few paid any attention to their assignments until the day before the meeting, most report, "I called the guy, but he hasn't called back." "Okay, get it done by the *next* meeting." Assuming the calls get made, it has now been *two months* since you kicked this off and still no progress!

Consider the alternative. Suppose you meet with your team every Monday morning at 7 a.m. Too busy? No problem. Meet on *Sunday* morning. See, I have already established its importance. Now, at worst, your people will consider their assignments no less frequently than once a week. And since deadlines are given in terms of hours and days, not weeks, momentum builds accordingly.

Now consider the message—and potential for results. Assignments in the targeting program are to be completed just as quickly and thoroughly as those in customer service, teaching or mentoring. In the world of two guys and the bear, who is going to generate more business—an organization with a monthly targeting program or one with the Six Step Process daily, weekly, hourly program?

Don't expect quick results. It takes time to woo the best clients. Remember, targeting is not to be confused with responding to unsolicited proposal opportunities. You are not seeking, nor will you accept marginal clients just to win one.

The Selling Cycle

After establishing the necessary organization, motivation and targeting *processes* to pursue the best customers in the market, your next step is to understand how the selling process works. The process of selling is a sequence of events common to the sale of all goods or services. The selling cycle consists of five distinct, yet sequentially related elements:

- Detect or create buyer need.

- Alert buyers to your ability to respond.

- Generate opportunities to present solutions.

- Ensure selection and exploit opportunities.

- Deliver outstanding quality and exceed customer expectations.

Use Relationships to Detect Need

The key to sales is exploiting your business relationships. Everybody is either a purchaser of the goods and services you sell, a potential purchaser, or someone who influences that decision. These decision-makers and influencers are crucial to growing your customer base. How will you *detect or create need, alert buyers* to your abilities and *generate opportunities* to present your solutions? You must know buyers, their companies, the issues and those who influence the buying decision.

To do this, be visible in your business community and industry. Advertise. Attend trade shows, conferences and other events where buyers in your industry congregate to trade gossip and pitch business. This takes time, but it pays off.

When assuming responsibility for a merged office, I was fortunate to have the founding partner of the merged firm as a friend and mentor. He was known and respected throughout the community. At our first meeting, he presented me a list of the top people in the community. Over the next several weeks, he introduced me to each of them. For the next five years, those people became the source of our growth. Personally know those who buy or who influence the decision of the buyers of your goods and services.

I once had a competitor who was very successful at developing relationships. It was said of him that he would show up for the opening of a car wash. He was everywhere. He knew the CEOs of his clients, kept in touch and added real value. We were on many of the same civic boards. He attended every meeting prepared. He was polite to everyone. He made it a practice to introduce his clients to one another, or to mine, to their mutual benefit. He understood the relationship of quality service to the growth of his business and maintained very high standards. He was consistently respected and his business thrived. I had great respect for him, considered him a mentor and sought to emulate him.

He was an excellent role model. I learned by watching him. He once observed that I was his most serious competition. I consider that among the greater compliments of my professional career.

In the course of developing relationships, I try to be on good terms with everyone, especially those who influence buying decisions. Remember, as a leader of your organization, you are always on duty. Your personal conduct reflects upon the quality of your business.

Every night I ask myself, "Who did you alienate today?" And I pray it is only in single digits.

Relationships are like pieces in a puzzle. One of them will provide the key to unlocking a prospect from the current provider. Find them. Nurture them. Use them.

Existing Relationships
Create New Ones

The clients you now serve well are the best source of new clients.

It is most comforting to hand your prospects a list of people they know and say, "Overnight delivery? No problem. Don't take my word for it, call them" or "Oh, you don't get your tax returns until the last minute. Ask them when they get theirs." Can't beat it. The word soon gets around that there is one organization that provides real value for the money.

One morning, I received a call from a client we had won some months earlier. Because of our service, he had become a good client and friend. He was calling to request a favor. He was working with a small tribe of Native Americans who wanted to develop their reservation into a casino. He asked if we would provide them with financial advice. Of course we would. When a client asks for a favor, you oblige. As I was then moving to an assignment in another city, I handed this one off to one of my partners.

Some months later, as a result of our interest and our partner's advice, we won the account. It was worth it. That casino has since evolved into one of the largest Native American-owned entertainment complexes in the country. This multimillion-dollar account originated with a phone call from a satisfied client.

Select your relationships carefully. Be especially cautious of people who beat down your door to be your best friend. Several years ago, as the new managing partner of a large office, I inherited a relationship with a very assertive lawyer who had been a friend of my predecessor. He was not my kind of person, but I had difficulty holding him at arm's length.

Finally, the fact that he had been thrown out of his firm for unprofessional conduct hit the paper. This gave me an opportunity to sever the relationship. But he continued to press me to recommend his services. Incredulously, I asked him on what basis could I do that. "Just tell them that I'm a great lawyer," he said. When I responded that I knew many great lawyers who were not admitted crooks, he got the message. Pick carefully. You will be known by the company you pick—or by who picks you.

Here is another piece of advice—for life as well as for business. What goes around comes around. You never know. Today's antagonist is tomorrow's valued relationship. The next time you are tempted to give an obscene gesture to someone in traffic, remember, he's probably going to the same meeting you are—*and he's the prospect.*

The building of any business occurs one brick at a time. Each relationship and job well done is a key brick. Keep stacking them and over a reasonably short period of time, you will have built a real business.

Ensure Selection

You are now well into the selling cycle. Detecting need, alerting buyers to your capabilities and gaining an opportunity to present your solutions is important. But it is not enough. Once you get the opportunity, make the most of it.

The Value of Expertise

To ensure your selection, you must have expertise.

Be very good at what you are selling. The days of the generalist, back-slapping salesman with little product knowledge are gone. Today, those who represent your organization must know your goods and services. Such expertise is also critical to understanding the needs of potential buyers. Everyone views their business as unique—and they are becoming more correct. The only person who has half a chance of getting away with being a generalist is the boss. Everybody else had better be very good at something. This is referred to as *industry* or *product knowledge*—and the marketplace demands it as the basis for selection.

When, early in my career, we figured this out, we all became industry *experts*. In practice, the expert was anybody who could attend the first meeting with the prospect. Since I enjoyed chasing new work and was good at getting it, I found myself with clients in diverse industries. Needless to say, as to industry expertise, I was a mile wide and an inch deep. Fortunately, I soon became a boss—a great position, where nobody expects you to know much of anything, and where smart people are around to bail you out. Provided you are smart enough to nurture and use them.

I stumbled upon the *value* of industry expertise while trying to solve another problem. As the new managing partner of a troubled office, I needed a strategy to unite a dysfunctional partnership.

Our SWOT Analysis indicated alignment between the major industries in our marketplace, our clients and our expertise. Industry expertise therefore became our practice strategy. Responsibility for client service, resources development and business growth was assigned to practice leaders along industry lines. This provided the infrastructure through which we implemented the Six Step Process.

Within less time than expected, morale increased and internal competition decreased. Everyone began to view themselves as unique contributors to achieving common objectives. Industry focus improved the quality of our training. As we began to understand client businesses, service improved. We became known for our expertise. When talking to a prospective client, I knew that nobody in town was as good in the industry as the partner sitting beside me.

Did it work? One morning, I received a call from an attorney for a software company to whom he had introduced another firm. Embarrassed that tax advice this firm had provided had proven incorrect, he recalled that I recently mentioned the name of one of my tax partners, an expert in software tax issues. We won the client. It was the beginning of a long, beneficial relationship–both with the influencer, his firm, the client and its senior executives.

The value of expertise manifested itself again one afternoon when my real estate partner and I were in a conference room full of lawyers and bankers. We were being considered as accountants for the creditors' committee in the bankruptcy of a large real estate development company. As we were making our pitch, someone asked my partner, "How do we know that you really understand these very complicated real estate deals?"

My partner rose slowly to his feet. He said, "Let me tell you what my idea of fun is. It's sitting around my pool on a Sunday afternoon with my earphones on, listening to classical music, while I read real estate syndication offering circulars. I understand their deals better than they do. Ask me any question about any of them." The black suits stared at him in silence—and soon selected us to perform the assignment.

Several years later, long after I had left town, another firm was considering resigning from all clients in a certain industry, due to perceived risk.

My successor as managing partner, a principled leader and friend, called his counterpart and asked him for some insight as to which, if any, we should approach. He laughed and responded, "Why are you asking me? Your guy knows more about them than we do."

Expertise counts.

Understand the Issues

Establishing a relationship is not enough. To win, the relationship must add value. Having identified buyers, to ensure your selection, you must understand their spoken—and unspoken—problems. Then use your expertise to develop viable solutions.

It takes more than the relationship. Our firm once added a valuable client which, at the time, was an important client of a competitor. The relationship between that firm and the client was considered virtually untouchable, as the CEO and the managing partner had been friends since childhood. They met at least twice a week at an athletic club for handball and dinner. Yet the managing partner of our office in that town—I'm not the hero of this story—determined that the company had a number of operating issues. Through the Chief Financial Officer (CFO), he raised questions and began to provide well-received advice.

Within a matter of months, we won the account.

Needless to say, the managing partner was crushed. "How could you do this to me?" he wailed.

"Well," responded his CEO friend, "In all the times we have been together, you never inquired into my business, asked how you could be helpful, raised any questions or offered any advice. I had no reason to believe that you cared. In fact, I began to think you were taking me for granted."

Demonstrate your ability. In getting to know a prospective client, our tax colleagues noted that the 1120 Federal Corporate tax return, as filed, contained an error. When corrected, the prospect would receive a significant refund. We eagerly waited for the moment when we could proudly announce our findings.

We were crestfallen when we gave the prospect the good news. He smiled and said, "Your competitor was out here yesterday and made the same point. Only they dropped off the amended tax return. All I had to do was mail it, which I did this morning, just before I called to give them my business." I never made that mistake again—and neither should you.

Understand the issues. As a young partner, I led an effort to win the business of a large, multicity communications company. Knowing that the prospect intended to consolidate operations in our city, I decided that consolidation was the key issue. So, working with their senior executives, I created a consolidation plan.

Unfortunately, we didn't get the work. While I was focusing on *my* definition of the problem, our competitor determined the CEO's definition. He learned that the CEO decision-maker lacked sufficient banking relationships. The CEO found my consolidation plan to be of little interest. But meeting the CEO's of every major bank in town was of great interest. It didn't help my shattered ego to find that my competitor successfully implemented my plan. Not understanding the issues is another mistake I learned to avoid.

Getting to the decision-maker is only the first step. Once you're there, make sure you solve the right problem and demonstrate real value to the buyer. With every prospective customer, pour on the service. Treat them as you would the best customer in your portfolio, because when you do, the odds are they soon will be.

Understand the selling cycle. Develop *processes* to respond to each element in the cycle. Develop and use relationships to detect need and gain access to prospects. Develop expertise and use it to understand business issues. Then respond with solutions.

And once you get the client, exceed expectations.

CHECKPOINTS on the Road to Heaven

Congratulations. You are now well down the road to Heaven. In getting this far, you have left most organizations—those who do not understand the Six Step Process—in the potholes of failure.

You are executing your plan by improving the effectiveness of business processes that drive the value of your people, their leadership and your customer base. Execution is the culmination of all of your efforts to motivate people and to create a values-based community, as well as the leadership it requires and your development of a viable strategic plan.

You are to be commended, but you are only at Heaven's doorstep. Before moving to the final Step—

continuous improvement—let's review the lessons of this chapter:

Your customer base is a primary value driver.

- How does it measure up?
- Does it facilitate achieving excellence?
- Does every customer provide the return that justifies your investment in resources?
- How do you know this?
- What processes do you have in place to answer these questions?

To enhance the excellence of the customer-base value driver, evaluate customers in terms of:

- Economic value
- Business risk
- Intellectual content
- Your difficulty in serving
- Any other value-based criteria

Based upon your answers, place them in one of four categories:

- The top 20 percent are *crown jewels* and must be retained.
- The second 40 percent are *good* and worth the effort to improve.
- The third 25 percent are *marginal*—either improve, or cull.
- The final 15 percent are to be *culled* immediately.

You will find correlations between risk and economics. Your low-margin customer is more demanding, creates higher risk and is less loyal. Manage the content of your customer base. Excellence only works with excellence.

Your existing customers are the best, least costly source of business. They also provide the necessary platform for growth. Answer these questions:

- Are your customers satisfied with your service?

- How do you know? Through surveys? Visits? How often? How substantive?

- How well do you understand their problems and business issues?

- What solutions have you proposed?

- What could you do better?

- Have you considered re-proposing to your existing customers?

- Are you content to wait for a competitor to do so?

- What processes do you have in place to monitor service?

If you are not serving your customers, you are at risk to an aggressive competitor.

You cannot begin to add new customers until you stabilize your existing customer base.

No business achieves long-term excellence without growth. You must add new customers. Begin by understanding the selling cycle common to the sale of all goods and services. The selling cycle consists of these elements:

- Detect or create buyer need.

- Alert buyer to your firm's ability to respond.

- Generate opportunities to present solutions.

- Ensure selection and exploit opportunities.

- Deliver outstanding quality and exceed customer expectations.

Everybody is a customer, a potential customer or someone who influences that decision. To *detect or create need, alert buyers* to your abilities and *generate opportunities* to present your solutions, know the buyers and those who influence the buying decision. Answer these questions:

- Do you know decision-makers in your industry and marketplace?

- How often do you attend conferences, trade shows and other events where buyers gather?

- Are you and your organization known to them?

- Do you monitor relationships and evaluate how they could help grow the business?

- Is everyone in your organization involved with selling?

- Do you target specific prospective customers?

- Do you have processes in place to manage the addition of new customers?

There is one more lesson to be drawn from a targeting strategy. Your crown jewels are at the top of someone else's target list. No matter how exciting the chase, never lose sight of the customers you have.

Relationships are important in establishing contact. But relationships are not enough. To win, a relationship must add value. Ensure your selection by understanding the issues and providing solutions.

Answer these questions:

- Are you developing true expertise with respect to the products and services you sell?

- Is your selling effort organized as you go to market?

- Do you have processes in place to ensure that prospects know of your expertise?

When your answer to all of these questions is yes, you will be well positioned to enhance the value of your customer base value driver.

Before moving on to Step Six—achieve continuous improvement—it is time to summarize. Two case studies follow to facilitate your review.

The first case study illustrates the application of the Six Step Process in merging two professional services firms.

Place yourself in the role of the CEO and note carefully the sequential application of the Six Step Process. Review the economic benefits.

The second case study illustrates the universal applicability of the Six Step Process. In this study, a

new CEO is introduced to an underperforming distribution company. Place yourself in his position as he
leads his team to excellence by following the Six Step
Process.

Both case studies are hypothetical, yet are composite representations of my experiences. The most
important point to note in reviewing them is this—the
Six Step Process is universally applicable. If the Six
Step Process works in two dissimilar situations, it
works in *all* situations.

Case Studies

LSB&G Achieves Excellence

Cultures cannot be merged—they must be created.

This illustration of the Six Step Process assumes the merger of two professional services firms. The facts and assumptions are, of course, hypothetical. The results are not. They represent those that you should expect when you follow the Six Step Process to the Heaven of Organizational Excellence.

Picture yourself as Ira Best, the CEO in the case study. You either are, have been, or will eventually be in his position. Compare his actions with your own experiences. Consider the decisions he makes as he leads his organization to excellence. Note the sequence in which he applies the Six Steps. Note his team's reactions. Also consider the likely outcome, had the Six Step Process *not* been followed.

The Firms

Remember, Letz, Cheatem & Goode, consultants to Global Colossal Technologies, Inc.? Under the leadership of its founder, Willie Cheatem, the firm had once been an excellent auditing and consulting firm. Its consulting practice emphasized technology, strategic planning, change management and other margin-enhancing services. Its smaller, well-regarded audit practice was located mostly in the Midwest.

The firm had languished for several years under Willie's leadership. Global's CEO had been a personal friend of Willie's. Willie had assisted the CEO in implementing an ill-conceived change initiative, in spite of his partners' reservations. After it failed, Letz and Goode decided that it was time for Willie to retire. The firm needed to reorganize, geographically diversify and grow.

Strydefer & Best was another well-respected audit and consulting firm. It had thrived under the leadership of I. R. Best, known to his friends as Ira. Its strong and growing audit practice was located mostly in the East, with one office on the West Coast. Its consulting practice consisted of litigation support and forensic auditing. They also needed to grow.

Ira Best and Willie Cheatem were friends and had often discussed merging. With Willie's retirement, it was time to act. Ira called Willie in midsummer. Their projected merger date would be January 1.

The combined firms would aggregate about $1 billion in revenue, with $875 million of recurring audit and tax work and the remainder—$125 million—consisting of consulting work.

The Journey to Heaven Begins: The First Three Steps

The partners of both firms met to determine if there was sufficient interest and advantage to justify a merger. Their agenda included:

The First 3 Steps

Step 1: *Master change.*
The fundamentals—motivation.
Were their motives reconcilable?

Step 2: *Build a values-based community.*
Were their cultures compatible?

Step 3: *Lead more effectively.*
Leadership. This was not a merger of equals. Who would lead the merged firm?

They agreed that these issues must be resolved prior to merger planning.

Motivation

Margins at both firms were under pressure. While both firms were apprehensive, it was more pronounced at Letz & Goode. As profitability had been flat for several years, the economic benefits of the merger were eagerly anticipated.

The primary motivator during Willie's tenure had been greed. It had produced an internally focused, distrustful environment.

The Best firm, however, was motivated by pride. Ira's vision was to be an organization of excellence—one that strived to be best at everything it did. The Best firm did not always understand what it meant to be the best or how to measure this, but they were motivated to achieve it. Becoming the best appealed to the Letz & Goode partners' pride—a new and stimulating concept.

Building a Community Based on Values

The cultural differences were significant. Willie motivated by fear. His focus on near-term results had created a culture devoid of teamwork or investment. Few processes were in place to hire, retain or develop people. Turnover was high, morale low.

Willie was *the* decision-maker. His decisions, made with little input, were final and not to be challenged. He was not receptive to change. "If it ain't broke, why fix it," was his oft-spoken motto. Letz and Goode did their best to shield the staff from Willie. They were both highly respected. Their leadership had managed to keep the firm intact.

In such an environment, everybody knew what to do to stay out of trouble. They took comfort in routine. Innovation was relatively unknown. Practices, procedures and processes were relatively fixed. "That's the way we do it here" was the usual response to any suggestion of change. Willie liked stability. Change was viewed as threatening. The culture was an impediment to growth, profitability and staff retention.

The culture of the Best firm reflected values that Ira had exemplified over the years. This is how Ira summarized it:

"In our firm, every individual is empowered to do that which is in the best interests of our clients, our people and our firm and is consistent with our core values of integrity, teamwork, respect and responsibility."

The prospect of creating a new, large, growing, financially strong firm was appealing, but challenging to the Letz & Goode partners. They wanted the benefits of the merger, but they were not sure they wanted to change their culture to achieve them.

In spite of its appeal, the culture described by Ira was threatening to the Letz & Goode partners. It was *different*. It would require changes in the way they operated. Change was a threat to their hard-won security. They hesitated. The differences were *too* great and *too* threatening. Heaven may be great, but who wants to die getting there?

The Letz & Goode partners suggested that perhaps the cultures should be allowed to align naturally over a period of time. Ira said, "Perhaps we should stop worrying about our differences and focus on what we have in common. Ira pressed his argument. "Who in this room is not a man or women of intelligence and character? Who does not support acting with integrity? Who does not value teamwork? Respect? Responsibility? If we support these values, do we lack the courage to adhere to them? To exemplify them? To manage our business in a manner consistent with them? To lead our people in living them?"

No one argued. They had agreed that they were men and women of character. And, having done that, how could they object to running the firm in a manner consistent with character? Who could argue with integrity, teamwork, respect and responsibility?

From there it was relatively easy to agree to principled problem-solving and participative decision-making. Ira agreed to seek input on important decisions. They agreed that he—as the senior executive—retained the responsibility to make the final decisions, provided they were in the best interests of the firm.

Resolving the Leadership Question

This was not a merger of equals. Virtually none are. The Best firm was larger and more profitable. It had access to broader markets and had more resources. Ira was known and respected by his clients, colleagues and competitors. All considered him an aggressive competitor, but a man of character. He was tough, principled and fair. Ira often said, "You can depend on me to be fair. But don't confuse fair with easy." Those who knew him were consistently loyal.

Ira's leadership had initiated the merger. Ira's vision dominated his firm, as it would dominate the resulting firm. He was the obvious choice to lead. This was not contentious. The Letz & Goode partners were only too pleased to have such a person lead them.

The partners supported Ira's vision of being excellent. And they agreed that the strategy for achieving it was to be the best in their business. Ira said, "After all, what's the point of going through all this if it isn't to be the best? By working together, we can do it." The Letz & Goode partners were hopeful, because Willie had operated in a traditional manner. Discussions in that firm had gone only one way— down. And the only objective had been to "make more money next year."

It turned out to be an easy question to call. They agreed that the merger presented an opportunity to create a new firm, with a new culture. They agreed that the new firm would be unique. It would be values-based and exemplify the principles that Ira Best proposed:

"We are going to create the firm of choice to the best employees and the firm of choice to the best clients. We will solve problems and make decisions in a principled manner. Our core values—integrity, teamwork, respect and responsibility—will be reflected in everything we do."

With the question called, the partners agreed to proceed to more substantive planning.

The Journey to Heaven Continues

Strategic Planning

In late summer, the partners evaluated their environment by conducting a SWOT Analysis. It was comprehensive. Their conclusions:

Considerable combined strengths

- Their combined revenues would approximate $1 billion, making them the largest non-Big Five accounting and consulting firm.

- They were well-known and respected in the middle market, the largest market for their services.

- The merger would create a geographically compatible firm, with audit strength in the East and Midwest and a presence on the West Coast.

- Their consulting practices were compatible and comprehensive.

- They had solid senior leadership.

Weaknesses

- The merger process would be disruptive to their clients and staff.

- Their good people might be open to competitive offers.

- Margins were already compressed, yet they needed to improve compensation to retain their best people.

- Managing such a large entity would require a stronger management structure, with more adherence to process than either firm had previously experienced.

- They required capital to expand into new products and services.

Opportunities

- The new firm could differentiate itself—if they were visionary and decisive. This was a unique opportunity to do it right.

- They would be the largest firm in the rapidly growing middle market, one that the Big Five had difficulty serving.

- The larger base could provide growth options through acquisition.

- The larger base would give them a more stable platform for operational efficiency, for upgrading clients and people and to obtain financing.

- The combined balance sheet would support long-term borrowing.

Threats

- The merger was high risk. Survival was dependent upon decisive cost control.

- The merger must not fail. Each firm was individually vulnerable. Neither was large enough or geographically disbursed sufficiently to grow or to serve national clients.

As a result, they made a number of decisions. They agreed that there were no substantial impediments. The merger should go forward. The timetable would provide for picking the low-hanging fruit, while deriving more substantive, long-term benefits. They would establish a sense of urgency.

Market

They would commit themselves to the middle market—consisting primarily of smaller, rapidly growing entrepreneurial companies. This market was not well served by their large Big Five competitors. The firm intended to provide this market timely service and well-trained professionals. Their national size would provide the resources and challenges to attract, train and retain the best people.

Organization

They agreed to an operating organization. There had been some support for deferring organizational decisions. "We should take it slow—see how people react. Let the organization evolve over time," went the argument. "On the other hand," said Ira, "how do you implement change without an infrastructure to make decisions? Besides, if we don't do it now, when will we do it?" They finally agreed to reorganize.

Best would be the Chairman of an Executive Committee consisting of himself, Letz, Strydefer and

Goode. The name of the firm would be Letz, Strydefer, Best & Goode (LSB&G).

The Executive Committee would utilize a matrix to manage the firm. Letz would manage the geographical organization, Strydefer the accounting, auditing and tax practices and Goode the consulting practices. Each would report to Best, as would the CFO, Director of HR and Director of Marketing.

They agreed that other senior positions would be given to the most capable partners. This was a difficult decision. The Best firm could have imposed their will. The Letz & Goode firm assumed they would lose some of their better people, who would not have leadership positions. They realized that this would be the first test of their commitment to values. Their appointments would need to stand the test of logic.

Leadership

The Executive Committee agreed that there were twenty five key positions to fill. Ten office/geographic managing partners reported to three regional partners, who reported to Letz. Three regional audit leaders and three tax leaders reported to Strydefer. Six geographic and functional consulting leaders reported to Goode. The process for selecting these leaders was long and involved.

First, the partners were surveyed. Each was asked to identify potential leaders to whom they would report and explain why they should be considered. The partners were also asked to identify any they would not accept.

Second, career information of those identified was assembled. To ensure credibility, the Executive Committee appointed a three-person committee of outside advisors—one appointed by each firm and the third by both. The three advisors were a retired Big Five Chairman, a retired CEO and a well-regarded consultant to the industry. The Advisory Committee was to make recommendations for each position and the Executive Committee would then make the final decisions.

Finally, after a month of interviews, focus group discussions, debating and agonizing, the Advisory Committee made their recommendations. They were accepted by the Executive Committee. The slate was then ratified by the partnership. There were some disappointments, but basically everyone agreed that the best people—on the basis of character, experience and past performance—had been selected. The process also identified a number of high potential future leaders who were induced to stay.

Planning Decisions

With the merger date of January 1 now only ninety days away, the Executive Committee made a number of key decisions.

First, the firms would operate independently until new processes could be emplaced—beginning probably no earlier than June. Next, implementation committees were formed: Facilities and Geographic Infrastructure under Letz, Compensation and Benefits under the CFO, Accounting, Auditing and Tax under Strydefer and Consulting under Goode.

Second, each committee was given the task of determining by January 1, the processes for which they were accountable. These were their choices:

- The processes of one legacy firm or the other could be used as a platform.

- One could be developed from both.

- Neither could be used and a process had to be emplaced to create a new one.

Finally, they were given the January deadline to fit into this overall timetable:

- Key process decisions by January 1.

- New processes developed by April 15.

- Training developed by June 30.

- New processes implemented by January 1, Year #2.

- Longer-term processes developed in Year #2 for implementation on January 1 of Year #3.

- Continue implementing the Six Step Process.

The committees evaluated their processes against the directives of the Executive Committee and the January deadline. Committee chairmen met every Saturday to evaluate progress.

Best and Letz, as the senior partners, visited each office together and met with partners and staff to discuss the decisions, elicit feedback and explain the rules. They committed themselves, as the leaders, to core values and participative decision-making.

They also discussed setting strategic objectives. The feedback was supportive of becoming the best. As one partner put it, "After all, going through all of this to achieve anything less would be a great waste of time. We'll never have a better chance than now."

At each of these sessions, Best and Letz called the question. Support was almost universal. They each spent time with those who viewed the new world order a threat to their stature. In a supportive way, they made it clear that nothing less than complete commitment would be acceptable. The partners also reminded them that, as leaders, they would be held to *their* commitments and would be expected to lead by example.

Finally, they ensured that a partner met with each client to discuss the merger and the benefits of having greater resources to serve them. Either Best or Letz met with the CEO of every major crown jewel client.

Enhancing Value Drivers

The planning process next focused on the value drivers that would ensure the merged entity's success. The objective was to enhance business processes that would create excellence in people, leadership and the client base.

The actions taken by the Accounting, Audit and Tax Committee were typical of those taken by the other committees. On a bright October morning, Strydefer assembled this key team—six practice leaders—three from tax and three from audit. Their task was to define objectives and obtain supporting information. They agreed to the following:

- Have a new audit process and supporting technology in place by January, Year #2.

- To do so, they needed to select one of these three options by January 1 of Year #1:
  –the platform of either firm
  –a new platform created from the two
  –build an entirely new platform

- Compile a roster of personnel, together with their performance evaluation and career potential.

- Evaluate support processes related to hiring, training and retaining people, leadership development and the status of supporting technology. Make a recommendation with respect to going forward.

- Evaluate the client base of both firms by economic results and the months in which the work was performed.

- Identify potential low fruit.

Subcommittees were directed to complete these tasks by the assigned date. It was agreed that the Accounting, Audit and Tax Committee would meet every other week to review progress.

Identifying Business Processes

The Audit Process Subcommittee recommended that the Best firm's Client Service Process be adopted by April 1. The subcommittee also recommended that the Computer Audit Process System—which the Best firm was integrating with their Client Service Process —would be the technology platform.

The subcommittee was to train the combined staffs in the new procedures by September 30.

Every engagement was to be reviewed by January of Year #2, to ensure its compliance with the Client Service Process.

The Human Resource Subcommittee presented an analysis of the combined staffs by time in grade, time in the firm, performance history and potential for promotion. It was noted that at least seventy-five managers had been in grade five or more years. The subcommittee was directed to identify by April 1 those managers not qualified for promotion to the partner level. It was also noted that compensation was falling behind the market. Corrective action—as much as a 15 to 20 percent increase—must be effected within the next two years.

The subcommittee recommended a survey of staff to identify needs and expectations and to serve as a benchmark for measuring progress. They assured the committee that focus groups would be involved in policy, procedural and training decisions.

The subcommittee presented an assessment of hiring, training, evaluation and promotion processes, with a recommendation that current year training be limited to training required to implement the Client Service Process.

The development of appropriate training would begin in the fall, with implementation beginning in Year #2. New hiring procedures would be implemented in Year #2.

The Client Portfolio Subcommittee presented their analysis of each client with respect to rate per hour and realization by the month in which the work was performed. It was decided that rates would be increased across the board, effective January 1. To the extent that they were realized, it was considered low-hanging fruit.

This subcommittee was directed to survey the top hundred clients–about 80 percent of the combined revenue—with respect to service, expectations and recommendations to improve service. The subcommittee was also to evaluate each of these clients with respect to economic return and audit risk. High-risk clients were to be culled as soon as practicable, but the evaluation was to be completed by May 1.

The Journey to Heaven Continues: Execute Your Plan

These recommendations were converted to action plans, which were executed beginning January 1. The execution phase of the Six Step Process, which continued over the next thirty-six months, substantially achieved the merger's strategic objectives.

Attention focused on improving business processes that enhanced the quality of the primary value drivers—people, leadership and the client base. As the firm focused on better university programs, the quality of new hires improved. Enhanced training, development and evaluation processes improved retention. Improved quality resulted in greater margins. The client base was culled of high-risk, low-return clients. New clients were aggressively pursued.

Finally, LSB&G achieved improved economic results. The key factors that generated these results were:

- LSB&G was clearly committed to principled leadership. A culture of participative decision-making developed the atmosphere of trust required to make important decisions. The leadership demonstrated a bias for action.

- Their vision of organizational excellence guided decision-making. The key question was, "What effect will this decision have on achieving our excellence objective?" Clients, staff and partners who could not meet constantly rising standards were culled.

- A matrix organization facilitated communication and coordination of planning, action and management.

- The firm pushed the numbers and examined the facts. Decisions were logic and fact-based.

- The firm focused on their clients and their people. The partnership demonstrated its responsibility for leadership. Frequent surveys provided valuable feedback.

- The Client Service Process was becoming a way of life.

The partners were generally satisfied. The Six Step Process differentiated their firm. It was becoming the best in the business—the employer of choice and the firm of choice to the best. The financial results demonstrated the substance of the Six Step Process. In the world of the bear and two guys, LSB&G had the sneakers on and was running hard.

However, all was not well. The senior partners were concerned that the firm was beginning to behave as if the game had already been won. They knew how quickly it could turn. After all, look what they had accomplished in less than three years. Were their people, with their new confidence, becoming too complacent? Without continuous improvement, the firm would be vulnerable to competitors, who had begun to react to LSB&G.

The partners needed to ensure that any changes made were permanently embedded in the culture.

LSB&G had yet to achieve Step 6, continuous improvement—the perpetual motion machine of organizational excellence—and the final step to Heaven.

The stage was set. The leadership and resources were in place. The client base was stable and
profitable. Firm confidence and morale were outstanding. The challenge now was finding a way to
embed the concept of continuous improvement into
the firm's culture.

How to do it? That was the question.

The Six Step Process
Creates Financial Benefit

Before we respond to the need of LSB&G to
achieve continuous improvement, we must respond
to a question that you may have been asking yourself:
The Six Step Process is interesting, but does it make
money?

The answer is yes. The Six Step Process maxi-
mizes long-term profitability. Financial success is an
indicator of excellence. It also sustains excellence by
providing resources to attract, train and retain the
best people. The objective of the Six Step Process is
excellence. Balance profitability with the investment
needed to create and sustain it.

The primary measure of financial performance
is gross profit. In professional services, it is gross
margin per partner. The following factors *drive* profitability by enhancing gross margin per partner:

- *Fee structure:* The prices charged for services.

- *Asset management:* Maintaining quality in clients and staff.

- *Productivity:* The efficiency of the resources
  expended in production.

- *Leverage:* The ratio of productive and non-productive resources.

Profitability is increased by addressing each profit driver.

Success requires applying the leadership, participative decision-making, planning and execution attributes of the Six Step Process. Organizations that have not followed the Six Steps will rarely realize these benefits. Success requires making tough calls and relying on your leadership to make them stick. There are no silver bullets or easy solutions.

LSB&G: Economic Fundamentals

Profit and Loss and Basic Economics

The Profit and Loss Statement and the basic economic assumptions with respect to LSB&G are summarized as follows:

LSB&G P & L (Recurring Audit Practice)		
(Millions)		
Gross Revenue	**$875**	100%
Staff Comp	260	30%
Gross Margin	615	70%
S, G & A	215	25%
Other	100	11%
Total Expenses	315	36%
Partner Profit	**$300**	34%
Per Partner (000)	**$495**	
GM Per Partner (000)	**$1,025**	

- Total revenue is $1 billion. Total recurring revenue is $875 million.

- Total recurring hours are 7 million.

- Recurring staff rate per hour is $109.

- Staff realization is 70%.

- Staff productivity is 73%.

- Leverage is 8:1.

- There are 600 partners and 4,800 staff.

- Gross Margin (GM) per partner is $1,025K

Revenue Profile

The revenue profile of the firm, reflecting the base economics, is shown in Figure 1 in the Appendix.

Allocation of Revenue By Realization

Revenue is a function of realization (percentage of base rates received). At LSB&G, it is summarized in six different categories, ranging from 120 percent to 30 percent. See the Appendix, Figure 2.

Allocation of Revenue and Realization By Month Realized

LSB&G is a seasonal business. The revenue, by realization category, is shown in the Appendix, Figure 3.

Compensation Model

The partners were concerned about staff compensation. See the Appendix, Figure 4.

Compensation was the largest component of cost. And, due to the competitive market for the best people, it was increasing. The partners worried that they were not paying their best people enough to retain and motivate them to remain with the firm.

The partners realized that without adequate compensation, their best people would leave. When that happened, quality—and eventually the firm itself—would decline. They were also concerned about the high cost of staff compensation. Competitive pressures on margin were beginning to impact the partners' earnings. Something had to be done—but what?

Enhance Profit Drivers

The partners understood that to improve gross margin per partner, they must systematically enhance each profit driver.

Fee Structure: Revise Pricing

After reviewing the market, their work in process and the work on which they were proposing, they increased their rates 5 percent across the board. There were some negative reactions. Not every client accepted a price increase. However, the overall result was positive. The staff rate per hour increased from $109 to $114. Realization declined from 73 to 70 percent. The net effect was to improve gross margin per partner from $1,025K to $1,040K.

Asset Management: Cull Marginal Staff

Their next actions were painful, but necessary. They had been lax in managing their staff. With business good, there had been no pressure to cut staff. In reviewing the staff situation, several factors became apparent:

- At least 10 percent of new staff hires were terminated during their first year—most at the conclusion of their first January to March audit season. In effect, they had been hired, trained and terminated.

- Of the 1,000 managers on the staff, seventy-five had been managers for five or more years. They had virtually no possibility of promotion.

- Most newly promoted to manager were, in fact, still performing senior type work.

- The firm was losing too many good people at the senior level. The reason, they were told, was a lack of perceived opportunity to progress to manager and beyond.

The partners took action:

- They terminated the seventy-five managers who would not become partners.

- They also terminated the 10 percent most marginal staff at other levels.

- Work was reallocated—mostly to younger managers, who, in turn, had their work reassigned to seniors. Excess senior work was assigned to more experienced junior staff.

- Excess staff junior work was eliminated.

Effecting these reductions took time. Their managers had provided faithful service. Discharging them without finding them employment would be inconsistent with firm values. These former employees were also excellent sources of business.

Except for stress, the benefits were positive. Productivity increased from 73 percent to 89 percent, staff costs were reduced from $260M to $235M. Gross margin per partner increased from $1,040K to $1,080K.

The substantial improvement in staff morale was an additional benefit. Younger staff realized that if they were asked to leave, they would be treated fairly. The best people recognized the opportunities for promotion that were now available. Client reaction was favorable. They responded well to the enthusiasm and fresh perspective younger people brought to their engagements.

Productivity: Reduce the Peak

One third of aggregate practice hours were incurred between January and March. The firm staffed to this peak. During this period, they worked at about 130 percent of capacity—between fifty and fifty-five hours per week. Yet productivity—the hours charged to clients compared with total hours available—for the remainder of the year approximated only 50 percent. This pattern encouraged seeking work to "fill in the valleys." Not surprisingly, most of the categories #5 and #6 low-realization work was performed during this off-season.

The partners carefully reviewed the schedule of Revenue and Realization by Month and took the following action:

- During the audit season, no services would be provided for less than 73 percent of LSB&G's normal rates. The ultimate objective would be to do no work during this period for less than the premium rates of 120 percent, defined as category #1. This was a good place to start. The effect was to move categories #5 and #6 work to the April to June period.

- The staff was reduced to those necessary to serve the reduced peak demand at 150 percent productivity. While that pace was challenging, it was not unrealistic and would only last for several weeks.

The results of these decisions were pronounced and immediately apparent. Productivity in the busy season increased to 144 percent, and annually from 73 percent to 87 percent. Headcount reduction resulted in staff costs decreasing from $235M to $215M. Gross margin per partner increased from $1,080K to $1,110K.

To mitigate the effect of a sixty-hour week, employees worked a six-day schedule: twelve hours on Monday through Thursday, eight hours on Friday and four hours on Saturday. While still demanding, the schedule enabled staff to be home three nights, a half-day on Saturday and all day Sunday. This policy maintained staff morale and efficiency at reasonable levels during their most demanding time of the year.

Asset Management: Cull Marginal Clients

The partners evaluated every client for risk and economics and placed them in one of six categories. Not surprisingly, they found a correlation between adverse economics and unacceptable risk.

Their actions with respect to each category were:

- *Categories #1 and #2*. These crown jewels were not to be lost. A service plan was developed to ensure that service opportunities were identified and exploited.

- *Categories #3 and #4*. Economic results needed to improve on these generally very good clients. A plan was developed to do so through better planning and rate increases.

- *Category #5*. These clients were terminated —unless the economic and/or risk issues were satisfactorily resolved.

- *Category #6*. Immediately terminated.

Every engagement was re-planned and re-staffed. Wasted effort was substantially reduced. Junior staff levels were reduced. Those remaining were given more challenging work. Junior staff time had always been viewed by client CFOs as virtually worthless. Therefore, fee levels were generally maintained, in spite of eliminating these hours.

The result was to retain approximately half of category #5 clients. Remaining engagement hours were reduced by approximately 10 percent, with no substantial reduction in fees. The staff was reallocated to new work—at about 90 percent realization. Busy season staff levels were further reduced.

The results were an aggregate increase in revenue from $875M to $980M, and a further reduction in staff costs from $235M to $195M. Gross margin per partner increased from $1,110K to $1,310K.

Leverage: Rethink the Concept

Question all assumptions as you implement the Six Step Process.

The extent of leverage—the ratio of staff to partners—is among those assumptions that must be challenged. It is generally assumed that the more leverage, the better. That is true, however, only if clients pay by the hour. In fact, most fees are set by the market. It is not unlike your relationship with a building contractor.

"How much will my new porch cost?" you ask. How much time the contractor spends and who spends it—leverage—is his problem. Your only decision is which of several bids is most attractive. So it is with the market. With the market determining revenue, your competitor with a ratio of 7:1—seven staff to one partner—is more efficient. At a ratio of 8:1, all you are doing is increasing costs.

The partners reduced their leverage from 8:1 to 7:1. The staff had been reduced from 4,800 to 3,500. The partnership was now reduced by the 100 partners no longer required to serve a reduced client base. This was a difficult but necessary decision, if the pipeline was to be filled with better-trained, motivated and committed people.

The final action taken was to increase compensation for seniors and managers by an effective 20 percent, increasing compensation to $225M. In spite of this increase in staff compensation, the adjustment of leverage increased the gross margin per partner from $1,310K to $1,465K.

Results and Summary of Benefits

The partners had now achieved their objectives —their staff was better trained, better utilized and more highly compensated. LSB&G was becoming the firm of choice to the best people—and they were rapidly becoming the firm of choice to the best companies in the marketplace.

They learned a very important lesson in making these decisions: The Six Step Process makes money!

As a result of the actions taken with respect to Profit Drivers—Pricing, Asset Management, Productivity and Leverage—LSB&G achieved the financial results shown in the comparative Profit & Loss Statement, which is in the Appendix, Figure 5.

For purposes of illustration, the changes are defined as Year #1—compared with Year #2. But, in fact, they would be better described as annualized results prior to and after the completion of the actions taken.

In reality, it would take at least three years to realize the full value of the decisions made in the first year. However, positive results would soon be realized, as rates could be increased and marginal staff and clients could be culled immediately. Also, the Client Service Process would be implemented in Year #1 and would be felt immediately, although its full benefits would not be realized until the second or possibly the third year.

The LSB&G partners were particularly pleased with their ability to reduce the aggregate cost of compensation—yet provide effective individual compensation adjustments of 20 percent to their more senior staff.

The change in gross margin per partner can be attributed to the results related to each specific action taken.

Realization and Rate Per Hour

The net effect of the entire process of raising rates, culling staff and clients, reducing the work performed at the peak and deleveraging the practice is shown in the Appendix, Figure 6.

Reduced Leverage

Reducing leverage from 8:1 to 7:1, as LSB&G did, is counterintuitive in professional services firms. The traditional leverage model reflects the assumption that the greater the leverage, the greater the revenue. As has been seen, this assumption is valid only if the service provider can control the pricing for services. Since this is rarely the case, increasing leverage usually just increases costs.

The benefits of *deleverage* are significant. The most obvious is reduced cost. But there are others. LSB&G reduced the aggregate number of staff, thereby providing better experience for the remainder. That created a more knowledgeable staff. Their reduction in staff enabled the firm to increase individual compensation, while controlling aggregate cost.

The result was win-win for the major constituencies of the firm—its clients, its people and its ownership.

Summary of Compensation Cost

A comparative summary of staff compensation cost for Year #1—compared with Year #2—is shown in the Appendix, Figure 7. Note that aggregate cost has been reduced, but individual compensation has increased approximately 20 percent.

γ   γ   γ

There are substantial economic benefits to be achieved in following the Six Step Process. By effective planning, questioning long-held assumptions and being decisive, it is possible to increase compensation for individual staff members—yet reduce aggregate compensation cost. All you need to do is think—and then follow the Six Step Process.

CHECKPOINTS on the Road to Heaven

This case study illustrates the Six Step Process. It shows you *how* to achieve excellence by following these steps.

Here is how Ira applied the Six Steps:

Step 1: *Master change—the fundamentals.*

Ira understood that fear and anxiety permeated the Letz & Goode firm. He moved quickly to restore pride. Ira gave people reason to hope. He led them through the Valley of Death. The key point is—he moved quickly and firmly. Ira confronted the issues and reaffirmed his message of hope, pride and future benefit.

Step 2: *Build a values-based community.*

Ira knew that reconciling the two cultures would not be productive. The challenge was to create a culture based upon common values, not past practices. Ira focused on what they had in common. Their character would be the foundation of their culture.

Step 3: *Lead more effectively.*

Leadership. Based on his personal integrity, experience and vision, Ira was the obvious choice. He established an objective process for selecting a leadership team. Ira instituted commitment to principled problem-solving and participative decision-making. He reinforced the values-based culture and established its rules. Before entering the planning phase, he called the question of buy-in. The stage was now set.

Step 4: *Create a strategic plan.*

Ira had a vision—create a firm that exemplified excellence. To sell his vision, he used logic and appealed to pride. He then articulated a strategy— become the best in the business. His SWOT Analysis identified strategic objectives. Planning focused on primary value drivers and the business processes that supported them. He instilled a sense of urgency.

Step 5: *Execute your plan.*

The plan was consistently and tenaciously executed. Ira knew the value of momentum. He was decisive. He made the tough calls. He practiced participative decision-making. LSB&G executed their plan by enhancing the business processes that affected their value drivers. They changed the firm. They created excellence by achieving strategic objectives.

Step 6: *Achieve continuous improvement.*

Ira realized the need to move to the endgame. We will see if he succeeds.

The Six Step Process creates economic benefit. The results in this case study are representative of those you should expect. If you think they are unrealistic, cut them in half. They are still impressive. If you consider a $1 billion entity too large to be relevant, then knock off a few zeroes. The results will be comparable *if you follow this process*:

- Understand the factors that drive profitability:

  -*Pricing.* Maximize fee structures. Compete on quality.

  -*Asset management.* Enhance the value of your assets. Your people, customer base and others—inventories, technologies or intellectual property.

  -*Productivity.* Employ resources more effectively.

  -*Leverage.* Manage productive resources more effectively.

- Enhance margin by addressing each profit driver.
- Capture the low fruit, but focus on the future.
- Be consistent. Be tenacious. Realize that benefits will appear over time.

Achieving the results described would take several years. The first year would provide mostly low-fruit benefits. The next two years would see improvement, as the results of better planning, the culling of marginal staff and clients and the development of better staff become apparent. If three years seems like forever—all I can say is this:

You had better strap on those running shoes. That bear is getting close!

HlthCo Achieves Excellence

*The character of its people is the key
to leading an organization to excellence.*

Before responding to LSB&G's needs for continuous improvement, we will illustrate the universal applicability of the Six Step Process. This case study is set in the distribution industry. It is a composite of my experiences implementing the Six Step Process.

Our example is Health Distribution Company (HlthCo), a wholly owned subsidiary of Global Colossal Technologies, Inc. Imagine that you are Joe Goferyt, the new CEO of HlthCo, a company badly in need of restoration to excellence. Consider the circumstances and the decisions he makes and compare them with your experiences. Note his reaction to change resistance as he leads his team through the Valley of Death. Think about what you would do, were you in Joe's position. Also consider the likely outcome, had he *not* followed the Six Step Process.

Background

HlthCo has these general characteristics:

- Revenues of approximately $500 million. Revenues and earnings have been relatively flat for the past several years.

- National distribution through geographically diverse warehouse and sales facilities.

- About 50,000 products distributed to about 4,000 customers across the country. Approximately 80 percent of the revenue from the top 250 customers.

- Purchases made from 2,000 vendors.

The relatively new CEO of Global Colossal Technologies, Inc. replaced the previous CEO who, after building the company, floundered in implementing the changes needed to sustain growth and profitability.

Since its purchase, HlthCo operated autonomously under Bill Ladebak, its previous CEO, and his management team. In spite of repeated initiatives, Bill had not been able to improve operating performance. In a growing industry, sales and earnings were relatively flat. Clearly, a change was required. It was time for Bill to retire.

Joe Goferyt is one of several bright young executives brought in by Global's CEO. He is an assertive, well-regarded leader. For the past two years, Joe had been leading another subsidiary with revenues of $100 million. In that time, by applying a Six Step Process he had developed, Joe transformed the company from mediocrity to excellence.

Global's CEO decided that Joe was the right person to turn HlthCo around. It would be a big step for Joe, but the CEO was confident. In the past, Joe's approach had been consistently successful. If Joe could implement his Six Step Process in a $100 million entity, why couldn't he do it in one of $500 million?

Joe was pleased with the challenge. He believed that HlthCo, with its staff of good people, was fundamentally solid. It had great potential. All it needed was focus and leadership. He was anxious to lead HlthCo to the Heaven of Organizational Excellence.

Step 1: Master Change

Understanding the fundamentals—motivation. HlthCo was an old line, successful distributor of medical devices to hospitals, clinics and long-term care facilities. It had not undergone the stress of recent change. Its former CEO, Bill Ladebak, a passive, yet capable executive, had been in place for twenty years. The company had grown slowly, but steadily, over that time. Bill believed in consensus. He rarely made a decision without everyone being on board. He was nonconfrontational, preferring to let things work themselves out.

The prevailing motive had long been pride, to the point of arrogance. HlthCo was the largest company in its industry and had done well for many years. Their culture reinforced commitment to long-held policies, procedures and business processes. Years of success had convinced inwardly-focused executives that their way was best.

Lately fear had begun to replace pride as the motivator. For the past few years, sales and earnings had been flat and the company was losing its market share. HlthCo executives had reacted defensively, blaming each other and others for their problems. Now, with their bonuses cut and the CEO replaced, they were anxious and afraid. They had enjoyed a lot of freedom under Bill. Now they feared the unknown. Who was this new guy? What would he make them do?

Step 2: Build a Values-Based Community

Creating the new culture. On his first morning, Joe gathered the key executives. He got right to the point. "We could spend a lot of time talking about the past, but let's talk about the future. Before we go any farther, I need the answer to one question. Anybody here not a man or woman of intelligence and character?" With no hands in the air, Joe pressed on. "Good. Character will be the foundation of our new culture. We'll build it from there." The HlthCo executives did not know what to make of this. They already had a culture. Why create a new one?

"What are the values we share?" asked Joe. The conversation began slowly, as the executives struggled with the question. This was a path they had never trod.

"Well, we like making money," said one.
"Our people are important to us," said another.
"We believe in treating people fairly."
"We work hard."
"We like being the biggest in our industry."

With Joe's encouragement, they became more at ease. The list lengthened.

"We are ethical people."
"We work together to help our customers."
"We care about customer satisfaction."
"We value diversity."
"We support each other."

Joe let this conversation run until the list was long and exhaustive. He then led them where they wanted to go—eventually agreeing that integrity, teamwork, respect and responsibility encompassed the values listed. They agreed that none could be deleted. Therefore, they must be core.

"Anybody have any issues with any of these?" he asked. No one did, so he pressed on.

"Now," said Joe, "If we believe in these core values, let me ask you—Does the company live them everyday? Do we, as leaders, exemplify them? Are they the foundation for everything we do?"

These questions were met with silence. They knew the answer. He continued, "Since we are all men and women of character, let's agree how men and women of character run a business." That seemed reasonable.

The conversation then turned to living those values. Joe defined each, carefully noting the reaction as his colleagues contemplated the reality of what they had just endorsed. Everybody understood what *integrity* meant—not cheating on your expense report or your spouse—especially with a colleague. That had always covered most of it.

Joe watched as they contemplated life in which intellectual honesty would replace rationalization, self-centered argument and debate, where moral courage required acting in the best interests of the organization, where fact and logic-based decision-making would become the standard and where procrastination and deceit were not acceptable practices.

Life, he could see them thinking, was certainly going to change. Contemplating the essence of teamwork caused reality to set in for those who had consistently held their buy-in until their political flanks had been protected. Was Goferyt serious?

Will teamwork require me to implement decisions that I don't support? What if this puts me at risk? This could be a threat to my power. Does he really mean that I'm to help those competing with me for promotion? Is he serious?

With Goferyt staring at me, it is difficult to do anything but agree. After all, it is hard to argue that the organization is more important than individuals.

It's just that I've never thought or acted that way before.

Who could argue with respect—but practice it? In the hierarchical society of HlthCo, returning phone calls to subordinates was rare. What if they had a problem that required a decision? Making decisions was high risk. Why must we show up on time for meetings, pay attention and participate? In HlthCo meetings, "dual tasking"—answering e-mails and taking and making phone calls—had long been an accepted practice. If those speaking found this rude, tough. We have a business to run, and besides, nothing ever gets decided at these meetings anyway.

Commitment to responsibility was also disturbing. Responsibility was not a word often heard at HlthCo. Nobody could argue with it in principle, but in the world Goferyt was describing, how does someone duck a mistake or a failed assignment? In the HlthCo culture, as long as you had some excuse for failure, you got a pass from Ladebak.

At HlthCo, it had long been a standard operating procedure to let someone else take the blame for your mistakes. And making timely decisions was never viewed as a responsibility. Better to let events dictate the decision, that way you never had to take the risk of being wrong. Somehow, though, Joe doesn't look as accommodating as Ladebak.

Step 3: Lead More Effectively

Creating principled leadership. This had become a long day. The HlthCo execs couldn't wait for the bar to decide whether this guy, Goferyt, was for real. They thought, "What is he, some kind of boy scout or preacher who gets to tell everybody how to run their lives? We did a great job building this company without him. Who needs it?"

But Joe wasn't finished. "When you get back to your office, you'll find a book to read for your homework assignment. It's called *Getting to Yes*. Since we are going to be guided by its principles, read it and be prepared to discuss it tomorrow."

Morning came bright and early. The HlthCo executives had made a few inquiries. The responses were consistent. They had been told, "Yes, this guy is for real. And by the way, be sure and read the book. He gets real testy if you blow off an assignment. Last point. Don't be late for the meeting. He views it as irresponsible. Not good."

The next morning's discussion of *Getting to Yes* was focused and positive. After all, who could argue with the logic of confronting problems rather than people, focusing on interests rather than digging in over positions, inventing win-win options rather than pressing your own advantage, and insisting on objective criteria in decision-making?

But how could you be sure that everybody would play? Trust had not been a characteristic of HlthCo's culture. Joe responded, "Easy. Didn't we all just agree to be bound by our core values? Violating these principles would not be consistent with those values."

Hmmmm. He had a point there.

From there, it was a short step to participative decision-making. As Joe described it, "The leader— the one with the responsibility—must ensure that everyone has an opportunity to provide input. The leader is then obligated to make the best decision possible in the circumstances and explain its basis. Once made, everyone implements, in spite of personal opinions. If the decision is wrong or new facts appear, we repeat the process."

"Any problems with that?" Joe asked.

"You're saying that we're obligated to go along, even if we don't agree? What about consensus?"

the group asked. Ladebak never proceeded until complete consensus had been achieved. They were accustomed to endless debate before any decision could be made. The ensuring discussion reaffirmed that teamwork *did* mean putting the interests of the organization before your own. That made sense—provided the leader followed the script.

"How do we know you will uphold your end of the deal," asked someone.

"We are all bound by commitment to the same values," answered Joe. "Since I'm responsible for safeguarding them, I am accountable to you for my end of the bargain, just as you are accountable for yours. That's what trust is all about. As values-based leaders, we are obligated to create organizations of trust."

Who could argue with that?

Joe concluded the conversation by calling the question. He said it would be their first, last and only opportunity to buy in. If they were not prepared to support the values-based community and the principles it exemplified, this was the time to say so. He then addressed each executive in turn, asking if they were "in."

Though there was some squirming, everyone answered affirmatively. It would be a leap of faith for many and a real challenge for a few, but no one could find any logical reason to say no. And they didn't think an argument without logic would be well received. Joe had made his point and the question had been called.

There had been only one significant issue. Harold, who had a great deal of power, was considered a corporate bully. He could be counted upon to hold up a decision until satisfied that his position was secure. Harold was a "What about this?" guy who would cite an exception that disproved the rule. He was emerging as an obstructionist and had been the only one who had obviously not bothered to read *Getting to Yes*.

The matter came to a head when he took yet another call during a critical moment in the discussion. Joe met with Harold later that day. Harold was arrogant. It was apparent that he was accustomed to having his own way. Harold did not appreciate Joe lecturing him. Harold emphasized his past successes and suggested that he would be needed in the coming months. His threat was obvious. Unless he was allowed to act in his own best interests, he might leave the company.

Joe responded that when Harold had been in the discussions about rules, he had expressed support. Joe agreed that Harold was needed—provided he was part of the program. He cautioned Harold, telling him not to assume that commitment to values-based leadership would blow over. Harold had a decision to make. He must demonstrate by his attitude a desire to be part of the community.

Harold stared in disbelief as Joe asked for a book report on *Getting to Yes* within the week. Joe concluded the conversation by cautioning Harold against assuming he was indispensable. "The cemeteries are full of indispensable people," said Joe. "We'd miss you for about ten minutes."

Joe was not sure if he had gotten through. He believed that Harold was only a product of his culture and deserved an opportunity to learn.

Only time would tell.

Step 4: Create a Strategic Plan

The planning process. Strategic objective? Make more money.

Every HlthCo executive knew that. Why else would we go through all this? Joe knew where this conversation would end, so he asked, "If making more money is our objective, how are we going to do it? What must we do to make the most money we can possibly make?

"Well, we'll cut costs," said one person.

"We'll have to do more than just cut costs. We'll need to add more revenue," said another. "And that means we need to sell more products to more customers."

"To do that, we'll need more and better trained sales people," said the Sales VP."

"We also must upgrade our distribution systems and eliminate the waste and inefficiency."

"We should improve our service. As it is, we have too many backorders. We can't even serve customers we have. How are we going to handle more volume?"

"Where will we get customer service reps and how will we train them? We already have too many problems in that area."

After about an hour, making more money was beginning to look like a major problem. The fundamentals, *value drivers,* as Joe described them—the people, leadership and customer base—seemed incapable of supporting their profit objective. In fact, the more they discussed this, the more it sounded like there was much to be done just to remain competitive.

"If we're going to make more money, what are we going to do about our business processes—the ones we need to train our people, manage our operations, make sales and deliver products quicker, better and cheaper?" asked Joe.

When they answered, "We'll have to make them better than they are now," the logic door slammed shut. "If we need to become *better* in everything we do, why not become *excellent?*" asked Joe. "All we're talking about is degrees of measurement."

That was hard logic to refute. Goferyt continued, "Yes, why go through all of this to just get better? Why don't we strive for excellence? Why not become the best in the business? *That* will ensure that we make more money."

The HlthCo executives had long been confident that they were the best. But they were becoming doubtful. They said, "If we can't make more money without substantial improvement in our operating processes, how can we really claim that we're the best? And we know that our processes need work. So we can't kid ourselves on that one."

Before the day was over, they were excited about the future that Joe envisioned. They *should* be excellent. HlthCo had once been an excellent company. Why couldn't it be so again? Their old feelings of pride began to stir.

To achieve excellence required that HlthCo become the best in the business. That meant employing the best people, satisfying the best customers and supporting this effort with the best business processes. It had been a struggle getting there, but as Goferyt knew, it was always better to have tough conversations early. It never gets any easier.

Joe was pleased that the Six Step Process was on track.

Further planning involved an evaluation of strengths, weaknesses, opportunities and threats in their operating environment. The SWOT Analysis took several weeks and produced this summary.

Strengths

- With almost $1 billion in revenues, HlthCo is the industry leader.

- The HlthCo name is well-known and respected.

- The industry is fragmented.
- The customer base includes a substantial number of Fortune 1,000 firms.
- The product lines are broad.
- Purchasing power is underutilized.
- HlthCo is geographically diverse.
- The management team is experienced.
- The balance sheet is strong.

Weaknesses

- The company sells primarily commodity products.
- The vendor list is extensive.
- There is a significant amount of slow-moving inventory.
- Recent mergers resulted in different operating systems supporting the regional warehouses and branches.
- There are still cultural issues. Buy-in is not complete.

Opportunities

- Substantial cost savings can be realized by rationalizing our distribution system.
- Aligned operations could be world class —thereby creating competitive advantage.
- Redeploying human resources would solve many operational issues.

- Training of customer service people will improve service.

- Upgrading, reorganizing and training our sales force will yield substantial benefits.

Threats

- The change process must move quickly, yet not disrupt customer service.

- Competitors can be expected to react.

- People—especially in sales—could be vulnerable.

- Vendors may not cooperate in taking back slow-moving stock.

- While consolidating computer systems, control of the business may be lost.

Joe and the other senior executives agreed that the list, though far from complete, gave them a good place to start.

The first decisions were organizational.

Joe suggested that the *operating* organization should plan and execute any changes needed. The team responded that they couldn't both plan and run the business. "We're too busy." "We should create planning committees." "We would oversee staff people, consultants and our junior assistants, who would actually create the plan." "We'll do what we do best —run the business." "We'll wait for the right time— and then integrate their suggestions."

"The decisions that must be made are operating decisions," said Joe. "How do we define objectives, focus on value drivers, develop a plan, assign tasks, hold people responsible and implement apart from running the business?

If we create these committees, everyone will have two jobs—integration and operations. How do we effect change without people in place who are responsible for the results? Finally, what are we waiting for? What are the advantages of waiting? How do we know when the time is right? And what happens in the meantime?"

The following organization was created:

Joe defined a matrix that would manage all aspects of the business. Its horizontal axis included the National VPs—of Sales, Operations, Distribution and Logistics Management—or inventory control and purchasing. Its vertical axis includes the Administration—the CFO, Chief Information Officer (CIO) and HR VP, as well as the Regional Managers. The latter would be responsible for the operations, sales and client service within their respective geographical regions. All positions reported to Joe.

Joe also engaged the consulting firm of LSB&G. Ira Best had impressed Joe with his commitment to the Six Step Process. Ira asked, "Why would you hire consultants to help run your business if they can't run their own?"

Strategic plans would be developed around primary *value drivers*—people, leadership and the customer base, as well as the selling, operational/procurement/logistics and functional *business processes* that supported them.

A monitoring process was developed to oversee the completion of these assigned tasks.

Selling and Customer Relations

To be completed by the National Sales VP:

- Stratify customers by margin, risk, and growth potential. Stratify product lines and products. Improve or cull to the extent required.

- Survey major customers to assess needs, quality of service and concerns about the merger.

- Appoint a VP of National Accounts, reporting to the Sales VP and assigned the task of developing a strategy to ensure consistently high service.

- Develop a similar process with respect to other large customers.

- Develop a plan to improve our sales force and adopt a compensation plan based on performance.

- Develop a plan to improve our customer service processes.

- Identify customers with unacceptable margins.

- Coordinate with the CIO in making integration decisions.

Operations/Procurement/Logistics

To be completed by the VP for Operations/Procurement/Logistics:

- Develop a plan to consolidate purchasing and reduce the number of vendors.

- Identify slow-moving and dead inventory and determine how to eliminate it.

- Determine the most cost-effective process to meet customer delivery requirements.

- Determine the extent to which the regional network of distribution centers and supporting branches can be rationalized to maximize cost-effective customer service.

- Coordinate with the CIO in making integration decisions.

Infrastructure and Support Functions

To be completed by the CFO, CIO and HR VP:

- The CIO must consolidate technology-based information management and control systems. Specific attention is to be focused on

    –Customer order-taking and processing
    –Inventory control and management
    –Vendor management
    –Accounting and financial reporting

- The CFO is to

    –Review, consolidate and renegotiate service agreements.
    –The treasury function is to be consolidated.
    –Rationalize accounting and control processes.

- The HR VP is to

    –Outsource all noncritical activities, including payroll and benefits administration.
    –Develop a plan for rationalizing benefits.

–Develop a plan to upgrade processes for hiring and personnel management.
–Cull marginal employees.

The deadline for completion was thirty days. It was more than sufficient. Besides, Joe knew that if he gave them more time, they would use it. A sense of urgency was required.

The Management Team met every other Friday and Saturday to monitor progress. If they did not complete their agenda by Saturday afternoon, they would remain over Sunday. Little meeting time was wasted. They were learning.

Joe visited major customers to discuss the changes and assure them of quality service. These visits were well received. No major business was lost during implementation.

Step 5: Execute Your Plan

Plan execution. The plan was on track. More importantly, the principles of the Six Step Process were becoming ingrained. Dual tasking at meetings was over. People arrived on time, prepared to participate. Principled problem-solving was becoming routine. They were embracing participative decision-making. Joe made the decisions. But he did so only after everyone was encouraged to make their case. Joe demonstrated that he was willing to listen, but that he would not always agree.

Best of all, Harold was coming around. Joe had correctly assessed that Harold was a solid executive whose position created a sense of self-importance. In the tolerant atmosphere of HlthCo, this attitude had been left unchallenged until Harold's ego affected his judgment.

The Management Team was learning to live their values. They were experiencing the atmosphere of trust that resulted from intellectual honesty and moral courage in decision-making, the benefits of teamwork, the collegiality that emerged with respect and the power of taking responsibility.

Bright and early one morning, they reviewed progress with respect to the thirty-day tasks. With plans on schedule, Joe shifted their focus to plan execution. Generally, the tasks were to be initiated immediately and completed as soon as practicable. This is a summary of the implementation objectives assigned:

Selling and Customer Service

- Raise prices 3 percent immediately and another 3 percent in ninety days.

- Reduce order-taking errors to zero through training, technology support and employee upgrade.

- Establish a National Account Program to ensure a consistent high level of service to these value accounts.

- The customer base is to be managed, stratified in four categories

  –*National* accounts
  –*Regional* crown jewels
  –*Other* accounts
    Analyze all as to current and future profitability. Cull those that cannot meet our definition of profitability.
  –*Remainder*
    Either find a cost-effective way to service, or cull.

Operations/ Procurement/ Logistics

- Rationalize the distribution system of regional distribution centers and branches.

- Reduce inventories by 30 percent.

- Reduce our vendors by at least 60 percent, eliminating those with whom we cannot or choose not to partner.

- Effect employee training in all critical operating areas.

- Become world class in logistics within two years.

Functional Support

- Select a common technology-based control system.

- Combine accounting, finance, treasury and other support functions.

- Combine HR and consolidate benefit plans.

When last seen, Joe Goferyt and his team were on track to achieve their goals. For the most part, they were adhering to their timetable and confident that they would remain so. The business processes that affected each value driver were being modified, improved or rebuilt and then aligned. Even more encouraging was the performance of the team and —through their leadership—the entire organization. They were focusing on the best interests of their people, customers and shareholders.

Joe and his team would achieve their objectives and continue their journey on the road to organizational excellence.

I'll spare you the number analysis. I think you get the point.

It was to be a while before Joe would begin to focus on the need to achieve Step 6 of the Six Step Process—continuous improvement. Ira reminded him that this was in the future and he would get to it in time. And when he did, Ira assured Joe that he would be there to advise him. After all, Ira had been there.

CHECKPOINTS on the Road to Heaven

HealthCo's story illustrates the universal application of the Six Step Process. Though the industry and the circumstances may change, the principles do not. People are common to all organizations. Their motivation, character, intelligence and capabilities are assets that can be utilized to lead any organization to excellence. Joe knew how to do it.

Step 1: *Master change.*
Understanding the fundamentals—motivation. Joe knew that the HlthCo executives were anxious. He quickly moved to restore their pride, using it to motivate them. Joe led them through the Valley of Death with firmness and sensitivity. He confronted Harold's resistance. In doing so, he salvaged a valuable resource.

Step 2: *Build a values-based community.*
Creating the new culture. Joe knew the culture must change. He quickly focused on creating a new culture that could sustain change. He knew that men and women of intelligence and character thrive in a

values-based environment. So Joe quickly established it.

Step 3: *Lead more effectively.*

Creating principled leadership. Joe was a principled leader. Expecting no less of his team, he called the question. Joe demonstrated that there is no point moving to a planning phase if the rules of the community have not yet been established.

Step 4: *Create a strategic plan.*

The planning process. Joe envisioned restoring HlthCo to excellence. His team supported him. Joe's logic was substantive. As intelligent people of character, what choice did they have but to support it? Who can be against excellence? Planning addressed their value drivers and the processes that supported them.

Step 5: *Execute your plan.*

Joe's team executed their plan by upgrading and improving the selling, operational and functional processes that created value. In executing their plan, they achieved their strategic objectives. They were achieving excellence. They were becoming the best in their business.

Step Six: *Achieve continuous improvement.*

They were on track but would need Ira's help. First, Ira had to lead LSB&G there.

If the application of the Six Step Process in this case study seems too easy, let me tell you how easy it *can* be. I recently met with the management team of a struggling company. We quickly agreed that we were men and women of intelligence and character. Within an hour we had also agreed as to how we would run the business. By the end of the day, the low fruit was getting picked and we were on the road to excellence.

Most organizations are composed of men and women of intelligence and character. They are underutilized assets. As a principled leader, your strategy is to appeal to them. Intelligent people of character will respond to logic, facts and positive motivation.

The amoral will not. Cull them at the first opportunity.

Step Six

Achieve
Continuous Improvement

Achieving excellence is easier than maintaining it.

Now you are back in the role of Ira Best, CEO of LSB&G. You have followed his decision-making through the first five steps of the Six Step Process. Consider yourself in his role as you lead your organization in achieving Step Six—Continuous Improvement. Especially note the role of communication in making the case for continuous improvement.

The Challenge

The challenge of sustaining momentum preoccupied Ira Best as he prepared for the annual Partners' Meeting. Ira needed a strategy. They were becoming the best, but they weren't there yet. Complacency was becoming evident.

So was inconsistency. It was like being a ten handicap in golf. The ten handicap hits mostly good shots in a round, but won't become a pro—the best —until *every* shot is perfect. As Ira put it, "Those with no futures include dogs who chase cars, self-appointed stars and pros who putt for pars." Ten handicappers don't make the pro tour.

Inconsistency and complacency are a deadly combination.

A planning meeting was held about three weeks prior to the Partners' Meeting. The last thing Ira did as he left the office was put a book in his brief-case. His good friend, Pat McDonnell, had sent it to him some weeks before, with the admonishment to read it. But who has time? He had been too busy to pay much attention to anything other than the business. Ira was forgetting his own advice. He thought, "We're so busy doing it the wrong way, we don't have time to do it the right way."

As he settled back for the three-hour flight, Ira pulled the book from his briefcase and noted the title, *Built to Last: Successful Habits of Visionary Companies* —by Jerry Porras and James Collins.[18] He decided to read it. Besides, he was tired of McDonnell badgering him about it. "Gosh, Pat's a good guy, but he can be a real nag," he thought.

Ira and his partners eagerly anticipated the annual Partners' Meeting. The past few years had been good. Their firm had come such a long way that they had remarkably little concern about the future. After all, who would have thought they could have been this successful? All most of the partners were thinking about was how much golf they could play.

As Ira took the podium after dinner, the mood was relaxed and morale was high. Everybody settled back to hear the good news.

"Good evening, partners. As owners of this business, we have every right to be proud of all that has been accomplished. Earnings are up. We are hiring, training and retaining better people and paying them fairly. The service to our clients is generally very

---

[18] James C. Collins and Jerry I. Porras, *Built to Last: Successful Habits of Visionary Companies* (New York: HarperCollins Publishers, Inc., 1994).

high. We are culling out marginal employees and re-placing them with better. All in all, life is not so bad.

"But that's the problem.

"It's not so bad, but it's not getting better. According to our client surveys, our service is very good, but not improving. Our quality control reviews tell us that compliance with our Client Service Process, which was designed to ensure quality service, is not being consistently followed. And I need not remind you that Global Colossal Technologies, Inc., one of our oldest and largest clients, replaced us. Why? Inconsistent service. Their feeling of being taken for granted. The questions we need to ask now are, 'How many more Globals are out there?' and 'Is that how we are treating our clients?' And finally, our people surveys remind us that we are not living our values every day.

"This feedback tells us one thing—our momentum is slowing. We may be achieving our excellence objectives, but we're not there yet. Here's the problem. Unless we rededicate ourselves to improvement, not only will we *not* get there—we may find ourselves vulnerable. Now that we lost Global, you can bet that our competitor is thinking, 'Those arrogant jerks over at LSB&G must be getting complacent. They are ready to be knocked off.'

"Are they right? Are we complacent? Are we beginning to tolerate a lower level of performance? You're shaking your heads. Is it in denial? No? Then you must agree with me. So, I ask you—are we going to tolerate it or do something about it?

"On your way out, you will find the book that is going to get us back on track. It's called *Built to Last*, and it is one of the best books on the subject of change that I have ever read. Much of what you will read we are already accomplishing.

"But there is one key point that we need to learn. It is this:

"Good enough never is.[19]

"The true measure of excellence is never being satisfied with just being good enough. *To be truly excellent, we must commit ourselves to continuous improvement.*

"Enjoy the evening. At eight o'clock tomorrow morning, we are going to commit LSB&G to continuous improvement."

There was not an empty seat in the house when the meeting started at 8 a.m. Not 8:01 or 8:05—but 8:00. Attention to detail was another firm habit. As Ira had observed, "After all, if we can't meet our internal deadlines, how can we meet our clients'?" At LSB&G, being late or unprepared for a meeting was considered unprofessional. Doing it right the first time was a characteristic of the firm.

The Solution

Ira waited for the buzz to die before he spoke.

"Good morning. That book must have been good. The place emptied out early last night. Many of you told me that it challenged you to think about continuous improvement. Several others commented that there's not much in it that we don't already know. I'll give you this—there is *nothing* in it we don't already know. The question is, how well are we doing it?

"Let me ask you—Do we *live* the principle that good enough never is? No, of course we don't. Do we care enough about our people, clients and those who come behind us to continuously improve? Of course we do. Are we willing to pay the price to get there? I don't need to ask. You responded to the challenge of becoming the best and I know you will respond now.

---

[19]Ibid., 185-200.

To do anything else would be inconsistent with our values.

"When we get back to work we are going to launch *Project Upgrade*—the program that is going to win the endgame of organizational excellence—continuous improvement.

"I'm going to visit each office for a two-day session. On the first day, we're going to evaluate our performance. How well are we achieving excellence in our value drivers: our people—our clients—our firm?

"On the second day, we're going to define the goals that will drive improvement with respect to each value driver. *Good enough never is.* We are going to set and then meet stretch goals. And when we meet them, we'll set them higher. And we'll keep doing that until the concept of continuous improvement is embedded into the very core of our culture.

"I want you to think about continuous improvement. Think about the words, '*Good enough never is.*' An attitude of continuous improvement characterizes every individual and every organization that aspires to excellence.

"I have a surgeon friend whose '*Good enough never is*' story involves a young resident who was desperately trying to tie a bleeding vein. 'I just can't get it,' he kept saying. To which my friend responded, 'Fine, we'll all just stand here and watch this patient bleed to death while you fail.' Our tolerance for anything less than excellence would be just as fatal to the firm. Each person in our company must improve every day, with every client, in every situation, without exception. Being the best means consistently the best—in every office, every market, every engagement, every day.

"I have been asked, 'Why now? Why didn't we just do this at the merger?' After all, this sounds like the *being the best* strategy in the Six Step Process.

"That's a reasonable question. We probably could have launched Project Upgrade back then. And it would have worked—provided we had addressed the fundamentals of the Six Step Process.

"The journey to the Heaven of Organizational Excellence is akin to climbing Mt. Everest. Reaching the top involves getting to various base camps along the way. By mastering the Six Steps, your leap to the top becomes possible.

"So it is here. We're poised for the leap. Consider how far we have come. Do you remember discussing the mere concept of *striving* to become the best? Did we really have enough confidence back then to consider driving for continuous improvement?

"Organizations must learn to walk before they can run. They must measure themselves against standards, decide what to do, and then have the moral courage and self-discipline to execute. They must learn to compete, to change and to win. We've learned that, and now we are ready for the leap to continuous improvement—the endgame of organizational excellence.

"See you back at the office."

As always, Ira was as good as his word. Within a week, Ira and his team were conducting the road show working sessions. The partners embraced this project with the enthusiasm that had become their hallmark. The results were presented to the Management Team. With their endorsement, the goals were ready for distribution.

Ira communicated as needed with his partners and staff. E-mail had been invented for him. Ira also wrote a column in a monthly staff newsletter. He had found no better way to apprise people of recent events—and to constantly reinforce his vision.

His announcement of Project Upgrade was classic Ira. He had never missed an opportunity to reinforce the fundamentals of their strategy. He consistently followed his own rules for communication—tell 'em what you're going to do, tell 'em what you are doing and then be sure and tell 'em what you did. And Ira never forgot to tell them why. He wrote his own material. Ira felt the firm deserved to hear it from the person they held accountable for leadership. Some jobs just cannot be delegated. Communication was one of them.

Ira knew he could be a bit preachy. Sometimes, hammering home the same messages, he wore them out. Ira didn't care. He viewed leadership as a process of focus and constant reinforcement. He never shrank from it. Ira might be preachy and repetitive—but nobody could complain that they didn't know the program.

Ira could be a pain in the neck. But he was a leader they all trusted—and to whom they listened.

Here is an excerpt from Ira's monthly newsletter column:

News From Ira:
—Project Upgrade—

We Must Improve

For years, we've talked about becoming the best. We're now even talking about *being* the best. And in individual offices, markets and engagements, we often approach it. But being the best means being *consistently* the best in every office, every market, on every engagement, every day. Frankly, we do not meet the test. So, it's time to make up our minds. Do we strive to become the best or remain content with being *good enough*? We must commit ourselves to continuous improvement or eventually fail.

Let's understand what we're getting into. Continuous improvement means continuous *upgrade.* That means upgrading our clients, our people, the members of our partnership. You recall the steps we took over the past two years. We culled senior managers. We continue to cull staff. We culled clients that do not meet our standards. Finally, we removed over one hundred partners.

With that done, we all collectively took a sigh of relief. We're glad *that's* over. Well, I've got bad news for you. Continuous improvement means that culling, pruning and upgrading must become a way of life. If we do not have the courage to accept that, then we have no business aspiring to become truly excellent.

Here we go—Project Upgrade. We commit ourselves to establishing and *maintaining* excellence in all aspects of our business. We are committed to continuous improvement.

Beating our competition is not enough. We must *consistently beat ourselves.*

Measuring Progress:
Achieving Stretch Goals

Stretch goals must be established. When they are met, we'll establish new ones.

These goals are set forth below. As you review the list, think about how many are within our power to influence, compared with those that are more a function of time. Also consider their interrelationship. None of these goals can be achieved in the abstract.

Our Clients and the Marketplace

1. A client portfolio that reflects minimum risk.
  • Continue to eliminate clients that do not meet the risk or economic profile that we have developed.

• Reduce litigation cost—which is now in the millions per year—by 50 percent, within five years.

2. Serve our clients well.
• By the end of this year, achieve scores of at least 4.0 out of 5.0 on client satisfaction measurement surveys. Achieve scores of 4.5 within three years.

• Have 100 percent compliance with our Client Service Process, starting immediately.

• No substandard performances detected in our internal quality control reviews, beginning with this year's review.

3. Achieve superior growth.
• Continue to respond to our clients' needs. Within three years, increase our percentage of special services—compared with recurring audit services—to 50 percent .

• Focus on our *crown jewel* clients. Within two years, double our revenue from them.

• Initiate targeting plans sufficient to obtain work from the top twenty-five clients in each of our respective markets each year for the next five years.

Our People
1. Upgrade recruiting and hiring practices, to obtain intelligent, well-educated people.
• Within five years, recruit 95 percent of our hires from the country's top university programs.

• Each year, retain 90 percent of our number one category and 80 percent of our number two category people.

2. Improve training.
• Continue to invest in our core training programs.

• Add training in special consulting and technology, until it is the acknowledged best in the business.

3. Support employees with the best technology.
• Continue to invest in and utilize state-of-the-art technology.

4. Evaluate, develop and promote people.
• Comply 100 percent with our development programs—especially the Senior Manager Program.

• Align performance criteria and measurements with our individual annual performance evaluation process.

5. Increase compensation.
• Ensure that we have the best paid people in this business.

• Recover our incremental investment through increased productivity.

6. Arrange working hours that allow people to balance their lives.
• Have 100 percent compliance with a "Peak Season—Six Day Maximum" work policy, beginning immediately.

• During other times of the year, comply with a "Five Day Maximum" policy—a standard 40 to 45-hour week over no more than five days, ending at 5 p.m. on Friday.

7. Maintain employee satisfaction. The ultimate test of our success is with our people.
• Within three years, achieve a 90 percent satisfaction level on all categories of our annual staff survey.

Our Partners

1. Ensure a culture based on our core values.
• Expect 100 percent commitment to our clients, employees and the firm—and to integrity, teamwork, respect and responsibility—the core values upon which it is based.

2. Ensure partner leadership in all areas of the practice.
- Achieve 100 percent compliance with our Client Service Process, beginning immediately.

3. Improve partner training.
- Initiate a Partner Annual Development Retreat, beginning this year.

4. Improve partner compensation.
- Exceed revenue and gross margin per partner goals. Increase objectives each year.

5. Be recognized as the best firm.
- Within three years, be ranked as number one in quality by the faculties of top universities and the market, as indicated by accepted industry surveys.

6. Hold ourselves accountable.
- Integrate and align these firm measurements and objectives with our individual annual personal evaluation process, beginning this year.

Though you may consider these goals aggressive, how many are unattainable? Consider the firm we will have when we achieve them. Our firm will certainly be better than it is now. Consider where we will be when we meet—and then exceed ever more challenging goals. And the good news? We control our destiny! We can do this. Nobody can stop us.

Consider the progress we have already made. Project Upgrade has the potential to achieve even greater results.

Risk Mitigation:
The Ultimate Payoff

Project Upgrade is about quality, because our business is about quality. There is a cost associated with quality or, more appropriately, the lack thereof. Right now, that's millions of dollars in annual litigation cost. That's good money being paid for past quality failures—the price of serving risky clients, underinvesting in people and not adhering to quality control processes.

This cost is not fixed. We are no longer going to tolerate incurring it. Nor are we going to tolerate clients, staff or partners who create it. Project Upgrade is going to reduce that cost. Merely reducing it by 50 %—a reasonable target—is the easiest money we'll ever make.

We will aggressively implement Project Upgrade. We know that we get what we measure. The goals of Project Upgrade will be integrated with the objectives of our offices, practices and personal goals. We will be aligned from our objectives to our goals to our accountability.

At times, it may be a struggle. The challenges remain formidable. But our best days are ahead of us.

And they were.

Over the next few years, the partners of LSB&G substantially achieved their goals—and when they did, they redefined them. The firm culled marginal clients, people and partners—constantly upgrading their quality. LSB&G grew the business, adding millions in revenue from new, high-quality clients. It also provided better service to the ones it had.

Litigation costs were substantially reduced. The firm adhered to its values—strengthening the culture of excellence it had developed. LSB&G made tremendous progress toward becoming the firm of choice to the best people and the best clients. The firm became known for its commitment to quality.

And the firm made a lot of money.

I know LSB&G accomplished this because, for substantially my entire business career, I have been some version of Ira or Joe. I have had the privilege of leading teams in a variety of situations and industries, from start-ups to billion-dollar businesses, in successfully implementing the Six Step Process.

So, as that Colonel said to us on that long ago morning at Quantico—I say on behalf of Ira and Joe to you now—"If we did it, you can do it."

If you follow the Six Step Process to Organizational Excellence—understanding and mastering change, building a community based on values, promoting principled leadership, designing a substantive strategic plan, executing your plan by enhancing business processes, and winning the endgame of continuous improvement—you will surely lead your organization to excellence.

And, when you do—

Ira, Joe and I will see you in Heaven.

CHECKPOINTS on the Road to Heaven

Continuous improvement is another of the many buzzwords, quick-fix management fads that have usually failed. When discussing the Six Step Process, I usually hear groans when I mention it. Many people have painful memories.

LSB&G's story illustrates the reality of long-term change. Achieving excellence is not as difficult as maintaining it. Ira knew that momentum had slowed at the firm. A feeling of complacency was sweeping the organization. The war had been won. They *were* excellent. But Ira knew that to be truly excellent, excellence must permeate the organization. Creating excellence is a never-ending process, not a one-time event.

There is a temptation in any change program to declare victory at the first indication of success. Management seeks evidence to justify the effort. Those who resist seize on it in the hope that the change initiative is now "over." How often have you seen quality, efficiency or profitability initiatives get off to a good start, achieve preliminary success, slowly die and then quietly fade away?

That is the nature of most change initiatives. To ensure it doesn't happen to your organization, resist the temptation to declare premature victory. Understand that change does not occur until the *process of achieving change* is embedded in the very fiber of your organization. Persevere until that objective is accomplished.

That is why I call continuous improvement the perpetual motion machine of organizational excellence. It is self-perpetuating. Like core values, it will survive the inevitable shifts in leadership—provided you have achieved it.

Embedding continuous improvement in your company's culture is the final step in the Six Step Process and the last stop on your journey to the Heaven of Organizational Excellence.

Epilogue

In the Preface, I told you that this book was for *you*—a person of intelligence and character who wishes to create organizational excellence. I assured you that by following the Six Step Process, you would achieve your objective.

Congratulations. You did it.

By applying the Six Step Process, whether as a CEO, an aspiring CEO, a young executive or an entrepreneur coping with the demands of rapid growth, you met the challenge. You successfully led your people to the Heaven of Organizational Excellence.

Your organization—whether a Fortune 500 company, a not-for-profit, individual department, work team or entrepreneurial company—has become the best in its business. The press—from *The Wall Street Journal* to your company newsletter—cite it as an example of excellence. The best people choose to work for you. The best companies want to do business with you. Competitors respect your firm, acknowledging it as the team to beat.

You have won the endgame—continuous improvement. The perpetual motion machine of organizational excellence is now entrenched in your culture. You have also learned that there is a pot of gold at the end of the Six Step rainbow. You are making money.

You have much to be proud of. Look back to where you were and see how far you have come. Review the critical steps:

You began by restoring confidence and pride. Before, fear was the primary motivator. Fear of losing major customers, making mistakes and the personal consequences of making them. Your emphasis on positive reinforcement, celebration of small victories and encouragement restored confidence and convinced your people that they could improve. Throughout it all, your communications reinforced this message.

Your primary contribution was principled leadership. You set the example. You exemplified the standards of excellence to which your organization aspires. You learned to enhance your leadership skills by using them. Your leadership created the environment of trust needed to begin the journey. Without your leadership, your people would never have completed it.

An important milestone on the road to Heaven was your creation of the values-based community. Remember the morning you began this journey? You listened to colleagues describe the issues and what they thought should be done. You then explained your views of a values-based community.

You began by simply asking your colleagues if they were men and women of intelligence and character. You were not surprised to learn that they were. In fact, you were counting on it. Their character would become the foundation of your new culture. Such people respond to logic, positive motivation and the challenge of becoming the best. Only such people could lead your organization to excellence.

You challenged your team to act following core values—integrity, teamwork, respect for each other, and taking responsibility for their actions. In doing so, an atmosphere of trust was created. Problems were seen from the perspective of solving them, rather than assessing blame. Commitment to principled problem-solving—with its emphasis on logic and facts—accounts for much of your success. By far though, participative decision-making was your most important contribution.

You didn't always agree with points of view offered, but you always considered them. And your colleagues didn't always agree with your decisions, but they were implemented. The process worked.

People sat in quiet disbelief as you explained the empowerment inherent in a community of trust. Some were skeptical that such an environment could, in fact, be created, as it sounded too good to be true. When you finally called the buy-in question, seeking personal commitment from each member of the team, support was unanimous.

Some doubted that you would seek their input. After all, no one else ever had. But you proved as good as your word—much to the joy of most, but to the detriment of others. "A" players rallied to this opportunity to create excellence. You did manage to convert some of the "Bs," but were quick to spot the "Cs." Everyone knew who they were. They had contributed little but mediocrity. Terminating them reinforced others' commitment to excellence.

You organized your values-based community into a matrix of functional and geographic leaders. Your team quickly began to work together in running the business. For the first time, they had a mechanism to communicate and cooperate in order to balance national policies and local customer service. They did not always agree, but for the first time they had a *process*—and an incentive—to find workable solutions. The team began to view problems as opportunities, rather than obstacles.

With a values-based community and leadership in place, you defined best in the business objectives. Primary, strategic value drivers were identified —your people, their leadership and your customers, as well as the others, including geographic consolidation, sales force reorganization, inventory and accounts receivable reductions. The processes that supported them were identified. By executing a plan to improve your major business processes, objectives were achieved. Rather than talking about the change *process*, time was better spent executing a change *plan*.

You realized that merely achieving your best in the business objectives wasn't enough to get to Heaven. You learned that *good enough never is*. And, having done so, you are now experiencing the benefits of *sustained* excellence. Your people will never allow themselves to become complacent. They are committed to the perpetual motion machine of continuous improvement.

That is your legacy.

～ ～ ～

Thank you for reading this book.

As I end this, and wish you continued success in implementing the Six Step Process, I will tell you that, over a career focused on achieving organizational excellence, I have accumulated many mementoes, gifts and memories. There is one gift, though, that is more important than any other—and that is the voice that speaks to me as I look in the mirror every morning:

"You didn't always do it right—and sometimes it was painful. But over the years, every stressful situation you found yourself in had one thing in common—you always left it better than you found it."

I assure you that in applying the lessons in this book, you will experience the satisfaction of hearing that voice speak to you every morning for the rest of your life.

Appendix

LSB&G Economic Fundamentals

Figure 1:

Revenue profile

LSB&G Revenue							
Staff Positions	Staff Num	Charged Hours	Total Hours	Full Rates	Real %	Rates Per Hr	Actual Revenue
Partner	600	1,000	600	$325	90%	$293	$175
Managers	1,000	1,800	1,800	$250	85%	$213	$382
Seniors	1,500	1,500	2,250	$150	80%	$120	$270
Staff	2,300	1,025	2,357	$ 90	22%	$20	$47
Tot Staff	4,800	1,335	6,407	$156	70%	$109	$700
Total	5,400	1,298	7,007	$170	73%	$125	$875

Figure 2:

Allocation of Revenue By Realization

Allocation of Revenue By Realization staff only							
Category	#1	#2	#3	#4	#5	#6	Total
Realization	120%	100%	90%	73%	50%	30%	
Rate/Hour	$187	$156	$140	$114	$78	$47	
% of Hrs	5%	15%	15%	25%	25%	15%	100%
Hrs. (000)	320	961	961	1,601	1,6	963	6,407
Rev (000)	$60	$150	$134	$187	$12	$45	$700

Figure 3:

Allocation of Revenue and Realization By Month

Revenue Categories	Period Revenue Incurred				
Period	Jan/ Mar	Apr/ Jun	Jul/ Sep	Oct/ Dec	Total
Composition					
Category #1	90%	5%	5%	0%	100%
Category #2	75%	15%	5%	5%	100%
Category #3	75%	20%	5%	0%	100%
Category #4	65%	20%	10%	5%	100%
Category #5	15%	25%	25%	35%	100%
Category #6	15%	10%	40%	35%	100%
Hours (000)					
Category #1	288	16	16	0	320
Category #2	720	144	48	49	961
Category #3	720	192	49	0	961
Category #4	1,045	320	160	76	1,601
Category #5	240	400	400	561	1,601
Category #6	142	98	384	339	963
Total Practice Hours	3,155	1,170	1,057	1,025	6,407

Allocation of Revenue and Realization By Month
(continued)

Staff Capacity Normal Weeks:					
Period	Jan/ Mar	Apr/ Jun	Jul/ Sep	Oct/ Dec	Total
# of staff	4,800	4,800	4,800	4,800	
Potential Hours (000):					
# of weeks	12	12	12	10	
Hours/week	40	40	40	40	
Hours per staff	480	480	480	400	
Total Capacity Normal Weeks	2,304	2,304	2,304	1,920	8,832
Staff Capacity Busy Season at 150%:					
# of staff	4,800	4,800	4,800	4,800	
Potential Hours: Number of weeks	12	12	12	10	
Hours per week	55	40	40	40	
Hours per staff	660	480	480	400	
Total Capacity –Actual	3,168	2,304	2,304	1,920	9,696
Productivity– Practice Hrs/ Normal Hrs	137%	51%	46%	53%	73%

Figure 4:

Compensation Model

LSB&G Staff			
Staff Positions	Staff Numbers	Ave Comp (000)	Full Comp (000)
Sen Managers	250	$110	$27
Ave Managers	350	$95	33
New Managers	400	$80	32
Mgrs	1,000		$92
Sen Snrs	450	$65	29
Ave Snrs	500	$55	27
New Snrs	550	$45	24
Seniors	1,500		$81
2nd Staff	800	$40	33
New Staff	1,500	$35	53
Staff	2,300		$86
Total	4,800	$54	$260

Figure 5:

Comparative Profit & Loss Statements

LSB&G Profit & Loss			
(Millions)			
	Year #1	Year #2	Difference
Gross Revenue	$875	$ 955	$80
Staff Comp	260	225	(35)
Gross Margin	615	730	115
S,G&A	215	240	25
Other	100	100	0
Total Expenses	315	340	25
Partner Profit	$300	$390	$ 90
Per Partner (000)	$495	$785	$290
GM Per Ptr (000)	$1,025	$1,465	$440

Figure 6:
Realization and Rate Per Hour

Staff Positions	Realization			Rate Per Hour		
	Yr # 1	Yr # 2	Diff	Yr # 1	Yr # 2	Diff
Partner	90%	75%	-15%	$293	$255	($38)
Managers	85%	96%	11%	$213	$269	$56
Seniors	80%	95%	15%	$120	$190	$70
Staff	22%	93%	71%	$ 20	$ 93	$73
Tot Stf	70%	95%	25%	$109	$161	$52
Total	73%	92%	19%	$125	$169	$44

Figure 7:

Comparative summary of staff compensation cost for Year #1 compared with Year #2

Note that aggregate cost has been reduced, but individual compensation has increased approximately 20%.

Staff Positions	Year #1			Year #2		
	Staff Num	Ave Comp	Full Comp (Mil)	Staff Num	Ave Comp	Full Comp (Mil)
Sen Mgrs	250	$110	$ 27	150	$132	$19
Ave Mgrs	350	95	33	350	114	39
New Mgrs	400	80	32	400	96	38
Mngrs	1,000		92	900		98
Sen Senrs	450	65	29	300	78	23
Ave Senrs	500	55	27	350	66	23
New Senrs	550	45	24	450	54	24
Seniors	1,500		81	1,100		70
2nd Staff	800	40	33	600	40	24
New Staff	1,500	35	53	900	35	32
Staff	2,300		86	1,500		56
Total	4,800	$54	$260	3,500	$ 64	$225

Suggested Readings

To better understand the management, leadership, decision-making and strategic planning principles inherent in the Six Step Process, consider reading some or all of these books—selected from the many I have read:

Ambrose, Stephen E. *The Supreme Commander: The War Years of Dwight D. Eisenhower*. New York: Doubleday, 1970.

Bush, George and Scowcroft, Brent. *A World Transformed*. New York: Alfred A. Knopf, 1998.

Collins, James C. and Porras, Jerry I. *Built to Last: Successful Habits of Visionary Companies*. New York: HarperCollins Publishers, 1994.

Daniels, Aubrey C. *Bringing Out the Best in People*. New York: McGraw-Hill, Inc., 1994.

Donnithorne, Larry R., (Ret.) Colonel. *The West Point Way of Leadership: From Learning Principled Leadership to Practicing It*. New York: Doubleday, 1993.

Fisher, Roger and Ury, William. *Getting to Yes: Negotiating Agreement without Giving In*. New York: Penguin Books, 1983.

Freedman, David H. *Corps Business: The 30 Management Principles of the U.S. Marines*. New York: Harper Publishers, 2000.

Freeman, Douglas Southall. *On Leadership*. Newport: The Naval War College Press, 1990.

Goddard, Larry. *Corporate Intensive Care: Why Businesses Fail and How to Make Them Succeed*. Shaker Heights: York Publishing, 1993.

Goddard, Larry and Brown, David. *The Turbo Charged Company: Igniting Your Business to Soar Ahead of the Competition*. Shaker Heights: York Publishing, 1995.

Goldratt, Eliyahu M. *The Goal: A Process of Ongoing Improvement*. Great Barrington: The North River Press, 1984.

Grant, Ulysses S. *Personal Memoirs of U.S. Grant*. New York: The Library of America, 1990.

Hesselbein, Frances, Goldsmith, Marshall and Beckhard, Richard, The Drucker Foundation. *The Leader of the Future*. San Francisco: Jossey-Bass Publishers, 1996.

Kissinger, Henry. *Diplomacy*. New York: Simon & Schuster, 1982.

Kotter, John P. *On What Leaders Really Do*. Boston: The Harvard Business Review Press, 1999.

LaMarsh, Jeanenne. *Changing the Way We Change: Gaining Control of Major Operational Change*. Reading: Addison-Wesley Publishing Company, 1995.

McCullough, David. *Truman*. New York: Simon & Schuster, 1992.

Maister, David H. *True Professionalism: The Courage to Care About Your People, Your Clients, and Your Career*. New York: The Free Press, 1997.

Manchester, William. *The Last Lion: Winston Spencer Churchill, Volumes I and II*. New York: Little Brown & Company, 1988.

Noonan, Peggy. *When Character Was King: A Story of Ronald Reagan.* New York: Viking Press, 2001.

Peters, Thomas J. and Waterman Jr., Robert H. *In Search of Excellence: Lessons From America's Best-Run Companies.* New York: Harper & Row Publishers, 1982.

Poirier, Charles C. *Advanced Supply Chain Management.* San Francisco: Berrett-Koehler Publishers, Inc., 1999.

Rosen, Robert H. *Leading People: Transforming Business from the Inside Out.* New York: Viking Press, 1996.

Sullivan, Gordon R. and Harper, Michael V. *Hope Is Not a Method: What Business Leaders Can Learn from America's Army.* New York: Random House, 1996.

Welch, Jack. *Straight from the Gut.* New York: Warner Books, 2001.

—And everything written by David Halberstam

About the Author

Pat McDonnell is President and CEO of The McDonnell Company, a firm that helps companies in dif-ficulty make decisive change. His entire career has been dedicated to helping businesses achieve excellence. He is an advisor, investor, educator, speaker and consultant for organizations ranging in size from start-up to those with over $400 million in revenues.

The author draws on a wealth of experience leading others—as a commissioned officer in the U.S. Marine Corps, search firm COO and, during almost thirty years at Coopers & Lybrand, in client service and office, regional and national management positions. For the last five years of his career, he was Vice Chairman of Business Assurance, the firm's largest line of business, with revenues in excess of $1 billion. Under his leadership, this practice was among the largest and fastest growing of the Big Six. After merging with Price Waterhouse, he served as Global Director of Assurance Services for the combined firm.

His expertise includes organizational transformation, change leadership, strategic planning, operations, finances, and mergers and acquisitions.

McDonnell received a B.A. in business from the University of Notre Dame and an M.B.A. from the University of Michigan. The author and his wife have three grown sons and live in Lake Forest, Illinois.

Pat can be reached by e-mail at:

pat@themcdonnellcompany.com

He would be pleased to hear of your experiences in applying the Six Step Process.